Unf*ck Your Business:

Stop Business Self-Sabotage by Getting Clear on Your Core Values NOW

By Tomas Keenan

*Unf*ck Your Business:*

Stop Business Self-sabotage by Getting Clear on Your Core Values NOW

ISBN: 9781072367918

Imprint: Independently published

Cover design by Sooraj Mathew

Edited by Hilary Jastram and Kathryn DeHoyos

Printed in the United States of America, First Printing, 2019

Dedication

This book is dedicated to those who spent their lives "in" their business and not with their true selves and families. I only wish you knew there was a better way.

Special thanks to...

Mom-
For always telling me I was capable of doing anything I set my mind to and to always beat to my own drum.

Donna-
For showing me what hard work and true professionalism is and much, much more...

Jennifer-
Since the day we met, you have fully supported me no matter how crazy my ideas and vision seemed to the outside world.

Thank you

Resources

To connect with Tomas Keenan:

https://tomaskeenan.com

https://topclassinstallations.com/

https://www.facebook.com/tom.keenan.988

https://www.facebook.com/tomaskeenan.tci/

https://www.linkedin.com/in/tomas-keenan/

https://clyxo.com/tkeenan

https://www.instagram.com/tomas_keenan/

Table of Contents

Foreword

I've had the pleasure and honor of working with over 16,000 self-starting entrepreneurs in the last 10 years. Some of them have won the Superbowl; some are on TV, many are multi-millionaires.

So, when I tell you that Tomas Keenan is the elite among the elite, I've got the street cred and experience to back up my statement.

In my trainings, I regularly refer to the work Tomas has undertaken. He's built a strong online community and bleeds for his industry.

When Tomas approached me and said he wanted to write a book, I knew whatever he put out was gonna be amazing. After all, Tomas isn't the type of person to do anything halfway. I know that he's personally poured his entire life's work and experience into this book. You'll learn about his trials, tribulations, and triumphs. You'll see a lot of yourself in the stories you read from this book. Tomas has a message and a journey unique to him, and it's worth reading about that journey to extract his wisdom from the lessons he's learned in life.

One thing I know about Tomas is that he's a massive imperfect action taker. He doesn't sit around and wait for the planets to align before he makes moves. He jumps in, head-first and takes action until the universe *bends* to his will.

In less than six months, I've watched Tomas cultivate a massive Facebook group, write a book, create an online training program, and manage his personal social media like a lifetime expert.

In all my years of coaching, I've never seen anyone do so much in such a short period of time.

They say if you ask 100 people if they have ever thought about writing a book, 100 of them will say "yes." Yet, less than 3% of the human race is the author of a book. The reason why is because writing a book takes focus, discipline, and committed consistent action. The fact that you're reading this proves that Tomas is willing to do what most are not. That's the reason he's qualified to write this book and why you should invest your time in reading it.

Enjoy the read...

Ryan Stewman
CEO BreakFreeAcademy.com

Introduction

There is no how-to guide or instruction manual handed to you when you open a business. If you want to speed up the learning curve, you'll need to spend a ton of time and money with a coach to work you through the process of adding structure to a company so that it can grow and scale.

I had to read dozens of books and spent thousands, upon thousands of dollars with a one-on-one business coach when I was several years into my second business being operational, so I could learn what I am about to teach you that is paramount to running your business successfully: Core Values.

Consider core values as being the navigation system.

I believe that personal core values define who you truly are and what you stand for. Company core values are there to define the company's character. This also helps to set the brand.

Getting clear on your personal core values will help you to determine your company core values.

Entrepreneurship and small business ownership is 100% the way to go to succeed, unlock unlimited potential, and become the best version of you. If you go to work for someone else or a big company, you can easily be held back as that person or business needs you to perform a certain role or task that best fits their mission, purpose, and pockets. I personally wouldn't choose any other profession. I'm at a point in my life now where I would never work for somebody else. If I did, I would probably be the worst employee on the planet because I have worked for myself for so long.

I started my first business when I was 21 years old. After spending years working for other people and learning everything I could and getting as many certifications as possible, it was time to step out on my own. I had $300 to my name, but I was determined to build something for myself. I worked on people's automobiles in my mother's driveway, out of her home, until I had generated enough money to buy the tools and supplies I needed. Eventually, I went out and found a shop I could rent, and I started to put a business together.

I jumped in feet first, even though I knew nothing about owning and operating a business. It's a whole different ballgame once you sign that paperwork and incorporate.

With this first business of mine, Exquisite Mobile Electronics, I was building some amazing audio systems. I was fabricating shit that I never thought I could possibly fabricate. People came to me from all over my area, some waiting weeks for me to work on their cars. I built a show car of my own and traveled up and down the East Coast, going to different shows, being requested by different companies, sponsored by different car audio companies.

The problem was I was doing all this cool, amazing work, but I wasn't making any money. I was the only person who could do it. I was the only person I trusted to go and do the work. I wouldn't trust somebody else to go and fabricate the panel, because I knew I could do it better. I wouldn't trust anybody to go in there and actually make the connections at the battery to power up the amplifier, because I knew I could do it better. I wouldn't trust anybody to run the cabling throughout the vehicle because I knew I could do it better. It took longer to teach somebody than for me to just go and do it myself. And that right there is the age-old trap of a small business owner, especially a technician within a small business.

I had fallen into the trap of the small business owner. I was working 20-hour days. My only focus was on the business and never on my health and fitness. I kept grinding and working so hard to try and make ends meet that my health declined.

At 25 years old, I had gained a tremendous amount of weight. I was 291lbs. I was on my feet for so long every day that I wound up developing severe sciatic pain down my right leg and all the way to my big toe. I ignored it. I wasn't making enough money to afford health insurance; so, I just focused on the work and tried to ignore the pain.

My fat ass standing on my feet all day and being so overweight, I wound up getting hurt badly with multiple slipped and herniated discs in my back. I could not walk for about three weeks and spent that time in bed. Finally, things started to heal, I believe, because of my age. My body took over and healed itself. But my back has never been the same.

If you do small business wrong, it can and will hurt or kill you: mentally, physically, financially, emotionally. It can wreck relationships. My first small business was definitely one of the deciding factors that wrecked a relationship with one of my closest friends—also my first cousin. I don't want to scare people away, because I know what I just said was a little negative. Honestly, if I had to do it all over again, I would. I look at my first business as being my master's program. Granted, I am not an educated person, but learning about business firsthand was such an eye-opener; it was so real, and it forced me to learn extremely quickly because it was learn or die.

No one told me about how to set up a business bank account. No one told me how to go out there and find a business loan, or how to hire employees. I had no one to tell me how to delegate tasks or develop systems and processes. I had no idea that to grow a successful business; I needed a clear purpose, mission, or core values.

Core values are important as they provide clarity and direction to your business. I look at core values as being very similar to marketing. Good marketing should not only attract the right people to your organization but should also repel those who are not a good fit. The way that you know that they align or don't align is by putting them up against your core values.

Once your core values are structured, and you've clearly defined what they are, you then use them to make any and all business decisions.

I'm a firm believer that what you put out into the universe is what you get in return. When you have clearly defined core values that you live and breathe every day, and make every decision based upon those core values, you're going to attract the right people to you and your organization.

What I hope you learn from this book, is to just take some time and get really clear. Figure out who the hell you are and exactly what you're there for before you dive in and start a business.

Chapter 1: Core Values

TOMAS KEENAN

◇◇◇

T here's a ton of information out there for entrepreneurs who are starting a business, but it is confusing to know what to listen to, and what will actually help you. Most of the information out there is how to structure your LLC or your S-corporation in your particular state. Do you hire an accountant or an attorney to do this for you, do you do it yourself, or do you go and use a service such as LegalZoom?

The first business I started crashed and burned hard, and one of the main reasons why it did was due to the lack of structure. Lack of vision is a big issue that many people won't touch on when it comes to starting a new business. Conveying my vision clearly to my employees has completely changed the day to day operations of my company, Top Class Installations, and this is in direct reference to core values. No one is going out there and telling new business owners, "Hey. You need to figure out or determine what your core values are prior to starting your business, or at least simultaneously as you're starting your business."

First, you need to determine exactly what your personal core values are.

If I had to open my doors all over again, I would have clearly defined core values in place before the first customer was ever served.

Figure out what you stand for as an individual, what you're willing to waver on, and what you're not willing to move a single inch on because you believe in it so deeply.

If you're going to list an item as a core value, it has to be in alignment with who you are, currently. It can't be wishful thinking of how you want to act or have people perceive you.

It really helps if you have your personal core values nailed down before you identify and implement your business core values because you realize what you stand for in life and the way you act as an individual. Lots of those core values can carry over into your business as well.

Part of the problem with new small business owners and entrepreneurs is that they don't take the time to structure these core values and they jump right in.

Once you have your personal core values in place, it's much easier for you to make these decisions when something pops up into your life. So, if something pops up that's not really in tune with your core values, it's a very simple decision. *Nope.* That *doesn't align with what I'm doing, what I'm attempting to do or build for myself, my family, my future, my legacy.*

The issue with jumping right in is before you know it, you're going to be so busy doing all of the other menial tasks and minutia within your business that you're not going to have any time to go back and get clear on your core values.

Before you get started tackling your core values, you might feel like saying, "That's a waste of time." "I have to make a sale," or, if you're a solopreneur and acting as a technician within your business, you might say, "Hey, I just made a sale. Now I have to take care of the fulfillment."

The fulfillment depending on the industry you're in could be boxing up a widget and shipping it directly to your customer. It could be building a tangible piece for your client. In my case, I might have to get into my car and drive an hour to a customer's location or a job site to work on their vehicles. There are many different ways that you can get stuck being the technician within your business and hashing out your core values is one of the biggest pieces of the puzzle that a lot of small business owners in the US, or even in the world at this point, are missing, and it is a huge, huge deal.

The beautiful part about using core values within your business is that there is no right or wrong way to do it.

I'm telling you, if you get clear on your core values, it will be a game changer, your life will change. The way you make your decisions will change, the way you hire your employees will change, the way you allow vendors into your life changes. The way you allow customers into your life changes, and again, this can also serve you in your personal life, but can also add structure to your professional life.

It's completely open-ended. Yes, you can share your core values with the world, and I do suggest that you do so, but ultimately, they're very personal to you. So, you can structure them any way you want. You can use words; you can use phrases; there are many ways to do it. I also don't think that it should take you years of soul searching to determine your core values. Realistically speaking, you can get clear on your core values in a few short weeks. I don't suggest rushing through the process. If it's something that's going to take four weeks or six weeks, just let it be. You're likely going to have to put the time in and think about it.

If you're into meditation, maybe meditate about it. If you're into whatever tools that you use within your personal toolbox to think about this stuff, just let it come through you and over time you're going to figure out what's what. The beautiful part about it is as you evolve as a person your core values change with you. I guarantee you that they will. You might add some; you might remove some.

I regard core values in a business setting as very similar to that of marketing.

There is also nothing wrong with leveraging or copying somebody else's core values, but what you need to make sure is that those core values truly align with you personally. One of the exercises I did early on was to see if people who I looked up to in some way, shape, or form posted their core values, whether on social media, in a book, or wherever. I found that some of their core values did align with my beliefs and actions. That's one of the reasons you will get along with and are attracted to these people. You want to be around them because your core values align

I'm not saying you need a 100% line up of your core values to their core values. However, when you are aligned with somebody's core values, whether it's in your business or personal life, you tend to click with each other. You understand each other very well. There's no bullshit.

I've always been taught that good marketing should not only attract the correct prospect or a lead to your company, or client, but it should also repel the people who are not a good fit for you. Core values should do the same thing. Your core values should attract the right people and at the same time, repel the wrong people. This is very true when it comes to hiring. This is also very true when it comes to dealing with customers, and again, also dealing with vendors.

Here are 4 ways you can utilize core values in your business today:

- Hire and Fire to your core values.
- Only do business with people/companies whose core values align with yours.
- Refer to your company core values while coaching an employee.
- Go over your core values during every company meeting to ensure they are deeply ingrained in your culture.

In my line of work, we subcontract for many larger international companies, and some of the relationships didn't take off. Over the years, we've taken a step back and, as a team, reflected on these different business relationships. The ones that work and the ones that don't. We look at each partnership from through the lens of our core values. It generally goes something like this: *Let's try relating each tough situation back to our core values.* Then we realized: *wait a second. Do you know why this didn't work for us?*

Because this company that we've been dealing with for X amount of years now, their core values don't align with ours, and they don't respect us. They don't respect our time.

Do your core values align with potential partners?

Whatever your core values might be, you have to look at the other company's core values and try to align them to yours, and if you don't have that tight fit that happens when gears come together and roll and rotate teeth into teeth, you're going to have major friction.

A lot of times you'll have to ask yourself: *Is it really worth me sticking with this company? This customer? This hire?* A lot of times, it isn't. Most of the time, it's a lot cheaper to pull the plug and step back.

Everyone should identify and implement core values

I learned about core values when I hired a local business coach. He guided me through multiple steps and stages of growing and scaling my business. I think everyone should identify and implement core values, but I don't think that everyone has the mental capacity or ability to understand the needs of having core values in place.

I hired my coach, Dean, and it cost me several thousand dollars per year. I would spend three to four Fridays a month in his office for anywhere from an hour and a half to three hours; I paid a shit ton of money to learn about core values.

If you walk into the corporate headquarters of most big businesses, you'll see their core values strategically placed within the facility for all to see. And if you're lucky enough to go to into a business that really gets it, you'll immediately feel the energy of the company's culture hit you like a shockwave as you enter and begin to interact with the staff.

But for the most part, when you go into a small business, you don't see core values on the wall. You don't get that warm and fuzzy feeling inside because they lack company culture.
The little fish in the sea haven't been privy to this information and what it can do for an organization. So, not only do I want to take some time in this book to give you the information to get started on your journey to develop your business core values, but I also want to open your eyes to how successful companies are leveraging culture to help establish and grow their businesses.

I'm offering all of my readers a free strategy session to help them kickstart their Core Values, go to: https://tomaskeenan.com/ and sign up.

TOMAS KEENAN

Chapter 2: Small Businesses Fail Because They Lack Core Values

TOMAS KEENAN

◊◊◊

Core Values are looked at by many as hocus-pocus; A lot of people think, "I don't need that." People respond to it by reacting: "I'm a big, strong guy. I don't need that stuff" Well, I want you to know, based on my experience of scaling my company from the ground up, you do need the structure provided by core values. They might just make or break your success.

Two-thirds of Americans dream of opening their own small business. This is recent data pulled from the Bureau of Labor Statistics in an article from Forbes, on June 19, 2018. This data shows that 20% of small businesses fail in their first year, and about 50% of small businesses fail in their fifth year[1]. Many small businesses are not managed or poised to thrive through today's challenges for a variety of key reasons.

According to Fundera, 20% of small businesses fail in their first year, 30% of small businesses fail in their second year, and 50% of small businesses fail after five years of being in business, and finally, 70% of small business owners fail in their 10th year of business[2].

---

[1] Caprino, Kathy. "How To Ensure Your Small Business Isn't A Failure Statistic This Year." Forbes. June 19, 2018. Accessed March 14, 2019. https://www.forbes.com/sites/kathycaprino/2018/06/19/how-to-ensure-your-small-business-isnt-a-failure-statistic-this-year/#1bf7040a73eb.

[2] McIntyre, Georgia. "What Percentage of Small Businesses Fail?" Fundera Ledger. March 20, 2019. Accessed March 20, 2019. https://www.fundera.com/blog/what-percentage-of-small-businesses-fail

According to Investopedia, the four most common reasons why small businesses fail are[3]:

1) Lack of sufficient capital;
2) Poor management;
3) Inadequate business planning;
4) Over-blowing their marketing budgets.

I would add a 5th to this list, though. A lack of solid core values.

If you don't have your core values established from the very beginning, it can be really hard to create them and put them into place later.

Company core values need to be very specific and actionable.

They need to help define your company's culture and show people the exact kind of behavior that you want to encourage within your organization.

Your core values should be clear enough to allow an employee to enter a tough situation and resolve it without them having to come back to you and ask, "Hey boss, how should I handle this?"

---

3 Horton, Melissa. "The 4 Most Common Reasons a Small Business Fails." Investopedia. March 12, 2019. Accessed March 14, 2019. https://www.investopedia.com/articles/personal-finance/120815/4-most-common-reasons-small-business-fails.asp.

Tony Hsieh is the CEO and Founder of Zappos. His quote describes the difference between personal core values and business core values. "Your personal core values define who you are, and a company's core values ultimately define the company's character and brand. For individuals, character is destiny. For organizations, culture is destiny."

These are some of the ways that you can test the values, some questions you can ask:

Can these values withstand the test of time? Twenty years from now, are these core values still going to apply? Will I still believe in them?

Will your team be able to easily memorize the values, yourself included?

Will these core values truly help you make better business decisions?

Can your organization stick to these values during stressful situations and economic downturns?

I think the most important one here is this:

Are your values aligned with your current behavior? Again, if your values are not aligned with your current behavior, it's more of a wish than an actual core value.

Have you ever walked into a big business and seen some shitty core values written on the wall? And then you have your first interaction with a few of their employees, and you quickly realize that those core values are just a bunch of crap and that no one truly believes them? I bet if you ask those employees you had those shitty interactions with if they could recite back the company's core values, I almost guarantee that they couldn't. That's a prime example that I've seen over and over again, of companies that just don't follow through with ensuring that their core values are implemented correctly throughout their organization, all the way from the shareholders, CEOs, down to the entry-level employees that they have.

Here are examples of how to implement core values into your company once you have gotten clear on exactly what those core values are. I'm going to give you some real-world examples of how we do it at Top Class Installations.

Example #1

At every quarterly meeting, our entire team gets around a conference table, and we go over our core values in full detail. This includes everyone from the longest-standing employee to the newest person hired a week prior. We sit around that table, and we get everything up on a projector, show a nice image of our core values, and we read through each and every one of them nice and slow. We make sure that we are continuing to educate these folks on our core values, constantly reminding our team of them.

Once we go over the core values, we then take a pause and ask everyone in the room if they could please give us an example of how one of their coworkers lived up to and exemplified the Top Class core values within their actions over the past quarter.

We reinforce our core values through continual coaching of all employees. So, if an employee does something really great and we get positive feedback from the customer, we will take that information and share it internally with a software called Slack.

We use Slack to quickly send messages to our entire team. This improves our "Communication," which happens to be a Top Class core value. We actually have a Slack channel dedicated to this.

The Slack channel is called *#RingtheBell*. If you see a message pop up in that Slack channel, you know it's going to be positive. We will then take the testimonial or positive response from the customer and post it in *#RingtheBell* for the entire company to see. What we're doing here is reinforcing the positive interaction by tying it back to our core values.

Example #2

At Top Class, we hire and fire based on our core values, not skill. We've designed a 7-Step hiring process that is designed to weed out as much of the bullshit as possible before bad hires come through the door.

We do this by creating hoops for the applicant to jump through. This can be as simple as giving very clear directions on where or how an applicant is to submit a resumé, what subject line to put in the email. We pay close attention to their communication and their reliability throughout the entire interview process, which is intentionally slow. Our interview questions are tailored so that the applicant's core values will bubble to the surface when answered. We ask several situational style questions based on real-world examples that we have seen firsthand.

Example #3

Continually evaluate your existing business partners, your business deals, your subcontractors, your vendors, anyone who you're working with outside the organization as well as inside the organization.

Example #4

Core values should be seen everywhere. From a PR or a marketing standpoint, you need to get them on your website. You need to let people who are searching your company realize that *this is what this company believes in*. If you go to, topclassinstallations.com right now, you'll see our seven core values posted clearly for the world to see.

I'm a huge proponent of social media, especially in today's day and age. Showcase your core values there, too. I constantly tell people, I don't give a shit whether it's your personal page or your business page, let the world know what you stand for.

Chapter 3: How to Identify Your Core Values

◊◊◊

There are two levels in identifying your core values; I call this the Hybrid System for Determining Core Values. What I'm sharing here, I did not invent. I actually pulled from two different sources when I determined my own personal core values, and so I have combined these two methods into a system and process that worked for me.

Level 1

Abundance	Daring	Intuition	Preparedness
Acceptance	Decisiveness	Joy	Proactivity
Accountability	Dedication	Kindness	Professionalism
Achievement	Dependability	Knowledge	Punctuality
Adventure	Diversity	Leadership	Relationships
Advocacy	Empathy	Learning	Reliability
Ambition	Encouragement	Love	Resilience
Appreciation	Enthusiasm	Loyalty	Resourcefulness
Attractiveness	Ethics	Making a Difference	Responsibility
Autonomy	Excellence	Mindfulness	Responsiveness
Balance	Expressiveness	Motivation	Security
Being the Best	Fairness	Optimism	Self-Control
Benevolence	Family	Open-Mindedness	Selflessness
Boldness	Friendships	Originality	Simplicity
Brilliance	Flexibility	Passion	Stability
Calmness	Freedom	Performance	Success
Caring	Fun	Personal Development	Teamwork
Challenge	Generosity	Proactive	Thankfulness
Charity	Grace	Professionalism	Thoughtfulness
Cheerfulness	Growth	Quality	Traditionalism
Cleverness	Flexibility	Recognition	Trustworthiness
Community	Happiness	Risk Taking	Understanding
Commitment	Health	Safety	Uniqueness
Compassion	Honesty	Security	Usefulness
Cooperation	Humility	Service	Versatility
Collaboration	Humor	Spirituality	Vision

Consistency	Inclusiveness	Stability	Warmth
Contribution	Independence	Peace	Wealth
Creativity	Individuality	Perfection	Well-Being
Credibility	Inspiration	Playfulness	Wisdom
Curiosity	Intelligence	Power	Zeal

Step 1: Determine Your Values

Using the list above, circle each value that resonates with you. Then hand out this list to friends and family who know you best and ask them to do the same on your behalf. After receiving the lists back, you'll notice that a few of the words circled will be repetitive. These values will take priority.

Step 2: Group Similar Values Together

Create a maximum of five groupings that make sense to you. There is no right or wrong here. If you have more than five groupings, drop the least important.

1	2	3	4	5
Accountability	Being the Best	Achievement	Caring	Knowledge
Dependability	Excellence	Ambition	Appreciation	Learning
Responsibility	Performance	Success	**Relationships**	Personal Development
Reliability	**Quality**	**Teamwork**	Honesty	**Growth**
Dedication	Consistency			Understanding
Flexibility	Service			
Versatility				
Commitment				
Trustworthiness				

Step 3: Choose One Word

Within each column, choose one word that represents the entire group to you. See words in **Bold** above for an example.

Step 4: Add A Verb

Add a verb to each bold word from Step 3. These now become your Level 1, actionable Core Values. See the example below.

1. Reliability	*Be reliable*
2. Quality	*Put forth quality in all that you do*
3. Relationships	*Build great relationships*
4. Teamwork	*Success requires great Teamwork*
5. Growth	*Enable growth in all*

Level 2

In level two, we are digging deeper with the attempt to learn more about what matters most to us. This is a process that asks some tough but important questions that will ultimately give you further clarity and insight into your personal values.

Step 1: Tough Questions

Answer these six questions. Take your time and be 100% honest with yourself.

Question 1:
What is most important to you?

Question 2:
What are you willing to do for success?

Question 3:
What are you NOT willing to do for success?

Question 4:
Besides making money, what else is important to you? Some examples: health, traveling, family, spirituality, etc.

Question 5:
List the most important people in your life and what you want to provide to them?

Question 6:
What personal values are you not willing to bend the rules on? This is you saying, "I am not willing to change my mind or my stance on this value."

By diving deeper and answering these questions, you'll further uncover much about yourself. This critical thinking exercise is a great mental workout. Don't get discouraged if you cannot answer all of these questions in one sitting. Take your time and let your subconscious take over. You'll know when the answers are there.

Step 2: Turn Those Answers into Statements

Turn your answers from the prior paragraph into statements. Go back to Step 4 and use the same technique here. Add verbiage to your answers, and you will drill down to your true Core Values.

Step 3: Live and Die by Your Core Values

At this point in time, you've worked so hard to get clear on your core values, to stop here and not implement them into your life would just be a shame.

Start by sharing your newly discovered Core Values with the world. Print them out and post them in areas where you can easily see them in order to remind yourself several times per day of who you are and what you stand for.

Wake up and read them aloud each morning upon waking and each night before going to bed. Memorize each value as if you were a student about to be quizzed on them the next day. Chances are you will be. Life will challenge you from the moment you wake up. Now with this super tool in your mind, you're one step closer to becoming unstoppable!

This now becomes the foundation for all decision making in your life moving forward.

You've built a really solid foundation for everything in your life moving forward at this point. You have your core values. Now you need to start applying them. When someone asks you to do something in life, you can stop and say to yourself, *you know what? Let me think about that for a second.* Before you say yes, take a moment and throw that question up against your core values and see if it aligns. If it doesn't align, you must, I repeat, you must say no. If someone asks you why, just tell them, "I can't do this because it doesn't align with my core values. It's not the right thing for me to do personally." If they can't respect that, then you need to get that person out of your life.

Everyone is aware that they hold some values. Without going through the exercise laid out earlier in this chapter and figuring out what your core values are, it's very difficult for you to put them up against the questions and the situations that life puts in front of you.

Although you might have these values in your subconscious and you might act upon them subconsciously, you're not guided if you haven't gone through the exercise and have determined exactly what they are.

If your core values don't match your partner's it's not going to work, period the end.

I hate to break it to you. It's good to determine this, especially if you're in a newer relationship with somebody. Do my core values align with this person now? If they don't align now, I guarantee you they will not align in the future. It's much easier to sever a relationship in the early stages than it is when you're deeply involved in personal relationships, marriage, kids, or business. Relationships can get fucked up real fast if you don't have aligning values. You will begin building upon a flawed foundation that will suddenly go to shit if you don't address misaligned core values early on in a relationship.

Get your business partner's core values hashed out because that's going to give both of you the clarity you need to get to the next step.

Let's say you own a business with this person, and you're 50/50 partners, that person should get clear about their core values as you get clear about your core values. Once the two of you have done that, then you can come together and work on the business values as a combined unit.

The business values need to overlap and be a culmination of both people within the partnership.

Still not sure how to get started finding and developing your own core values? Head over to https://tomaskeenan.com/ and sign up for a free strategy session.

TOMAS KEENAN

Chapter 4: Not All Work is Good Work

TOMAS KEENAN

◊◊◊

I dentifying your core values will eliminate the fear of saying "no" as a new business partner.

For many years I was afraid to say "no." I was taught that you take what you can get. Whatever work came my way, I said "yes," even though it wasn't always the right work to say "yes" to.

We're conditioned to believe that you must accept every bit of work that comes your way, that you must consider it a blessing. I'm here to tell you firsthand, that's complete bullshit.

When I first started in business for myself, I took anything thrown at me because I was hungry, hungry to prove myself to me, and to all who had doubted me in the past. This, unfortunately, was a time suck, a huge time suck.

Although I learned very quickly from doing this what was and what was not worth doing, and yes, it definitely improved my skill set in various areas, unfortunately, it wasted my most valuable asset, time, by taking my focus off the activities that would have helped grow my business faster. Because I said "yes," I now had to uphold my word, and complete whatever it was that I had hastily agreed to.

In many cases, I was doing work I knew nothing about. I was installing products that I had never seen, and I had to educate myself before completing the work, therefore wasting more time. If I had said "no," I could have focused on real business building activities such as creating systems and processes, hiring, marketing, et cetera. I could have even focused solely on closing more sales in an area where my company and I actually liked doing the work and were good at it. To take it a step further, we could have sold work that we were efficient at. We could have sold a job, and quickly, and efficiently turned that job out, and collected profit.

If I had only put a little structure in place before saying "yes" to everything, I would have avoided all of the work that wasn't a good fit for my company and me.

Saying "no" aligns with your core values.

Think of your core values as the doorman of a club. It's their job to make sure undesirables – in this case, clients that are a poor fit – don't make it in the door.

You need a way to filter what work you actually accept versus decline. Structure is needed so that when you assess the opportunity, you can come to a quick determination if the job or activity is for you and your business. Having the proper vision in place from the beginning would have greatly reduced the errors I made early on. If you don't know where the ship is going, how do you set the right course?

Determining why I was in business, and getting clear on who we served, and what we served them, would have made life so much easier. Having a clear determination of my company core values, and knowing exactly who we serve best, would have allowed me to evaluate the deals and opportunities presented before giving up the one resource you cannot make more of, time.

If you find yourself compromising with an employee who performs poorly, at what point do you decide to take action and get rid of this person? If you have your core values in place, you can now leverage them. You can put this employee's actions against your core values and say, "All right, did it align here? Did it align here? Did it align here? Nope, it didn't." And now you have a scale at which you can grade the employee.

Core values keep your team strong.

The process of re-identifying core values should be executed more often and better prioritized. So, as mentioned earlier, at Top Class Installations, we hold a quarterly meeting in which we have the entire team come into our office. We sit down, and for the majority of the day, we go over everything. Financials, core values, mission, purpose, a whole gamut of information is discussed.

One of the exercises that we perform at each of these quarterly meetings is what we call *Start, Stop, Keep.* We basically go to the whiteboard, and we write the title of START, and the question is asked to the entire room, what do we need to start doing at Top Class Installations to succeed in the next quarter, to achieve our goals at the end of this upcoming year? Once everyone has spoken, and we gain clarity, we go to the next exercise, which is STOP. We ask the question, "What do we need to STOP doing at Top Class Installations to succeed?" The third portion of it, is what do we need to KEEP doing at Top Class Installations to continue being successful?

We added this exercise to our end-of-year quarterly meeting in 2017. We had our team come into our office, and we got to the stop section of this, and we went through a whole list of different things. I had the bright idea to also dig a little deeper on this stop section, and the question was asked, "Who do we need to stop doing work for?" At this point, we had gained further clarity on our core values, and we realized that not every customer was ideal for us. The magic of this was that almost every single person in that room immediately raised their hands and almost simultaneously called out the same exact company. It was a company that we were subcontracting for, and honestly, they were a thorn in everyone's ass. They were difficult to deal with; they paid like shit; their customers were cranky, and it just wasn't working. Everyone simultaneously decided that this customer was no longer a good fit for Top Class Installations.

The importance of this is that we decided as a team.

This empowered my business partner, and me to take immediate action within 24 hours. We had a quick discussion after the quarterly meeting and said, "Everyone here in the meeting is right. We're all in agreement. Let's call up this company that we're doing the work for and notify them immediately that we can no longer continue to uphold our agreement and do work."

So, we made the phone call. We told the contact, "Thanks for the business, but unfortunately, we can no longer work for you." It was as simple as that. We knew immediately that it was the right decision because the person that we were speaking to on the other line didn't come back to us and say, "Oh my, you guys do such a great job. We really want to keep you on." There was congruency on both ends. They weren't thrilled with us. We weren't thrilled with them. Our employees couldn't stand working with them. Therefore, even though it was a loss in revenue, it was for the better.

Everyone breathed a sigh of relief the following day when we came back to the team and said, "Guess what? Remember you guys had mentioned that we should stop doing business with this person, and this company? Well, we made the phone call yesterday, and we are no longer doing work for them."

The immediate action that we took was very important to our team.

It showed them that the owners, myself and my partner, were supportive of their decision and that keeping a hurtful client on wasn't doing the business any good. It showed the team that their input greatly affected our decision to move forward and cut the cord on this person and this company.

We don't have that many customers, believe it or not. Yes, we deal with a lot of companies, which we call the end user. But our clients are only a handful. We have about 15 or so clients in total. What these clients do is they go into the marketplace, they sell the product, and then we show up and install the product that they sell.

This gives us a handful of people to look at as far as our clients are concerned. It becomes very clear when we're looking at this data, who is at the top of the totem pole, and who is at the bottom of the totem pole as far as revenue is concerned.

I'm sure most of you have heard of the 80/20 rule. It's also known as Pareto's principle. And the rule basically states that 20% of your inputs produce 80% of your outputs. Looking over the numbers, we could clearly see that this rule applies to us. We look at this list of customers, and we see who's producing what. It becomes very clear that the bottom 20% of these customers tend to contribute to 80% of our headaches. This is what I call reversing the 80/20 rule. Most people say that 20% of your customers produce 80% of your income, well, if you flip the 80/20 rule upside down, you can also say that 20% of your customers are shitty and produce 80% of your headaches. We go in there, and we look at the bottom half of these customers.

And at least once a year, and honestly, we should do it more often, we look at the numbers and we say, "Hey, who's the bottom 20%? And would it kill us if we stop doing business with this company tomorrow?" The answer's usually no.

Then we'll cut the company. We'll stop doing work for them. They'll stop sucking our time; they'll stop sucking the morale out of our team. Then we can take that effort, energy and time we were expelling on these folks, and apply it to customers who we align with, who are producing good revenue for the company and are much easier to deal with overall.

Solid core values make it easy to say "no" when the wrong work or partnership comes knocking. If you need help kickstarting the implementation of your core values, I can help. Head over to https://tomaskeenan.com/ and sign up for a free strategy session.

TOMAS KEENAN

Chapter 5: Systems and Processes

◊◊◊

In this section, we're going to discuss systems and processes in order to help you figure out if a client is a good fit for your business. If you have eliminated someone using the reversed 80/20 rule, how can you fine-tune your existing systems and processes to mitigate the risk of doing business with bad customers in the future?

Before we jump into your systems and processes, let me just get clear really quick. Most people get scared when they hear or read what I am about to say. But a system can be as simple as opening up an iNote on your iPhone or your computer and writing down the steps, step one, step two, step three. It could be as simple as a quickly printed sheet with a checklist. It does not have to be complex. You don't need crazy software for this. You need a pen and paper realistically, and maybe a photocopier, and you could have a checklist, or a system or process developed within your business very quickly.

Build a process that automatically disqualifies and eliminates the wrong people from entering your organization.

So now that you've eliminated people who have come through as customers and let's say cut the bottom 20% that are giving you and your team the most grief, it's time to take a step back and ask, "What are my current systems and processes? What's the current new vendor onboarding system and process that I have in place? What is the new hiring and onboarding system that I need to have in place? What's the new subcontractor onboarding system?"

Here are two examples of hoops:

1. Ask situational questions. If you don't get the exact answer your looking for, move on. However, this is where you can learn quite a bit about your company. Especially when you receive an answer that's outside the box.

2. Require them to complete an onboarding assessment. The goal here is to see if they can follow directions. It doesn't matter what the questions and answers are.

We have a 7-Stage hiring process at Top Class Installations. During stages 3 and 4, we post jobs on Facebook, Indeed, ZipRecruiter, Monster, or Craigslist. Most of those services have features built-in where the potential candidate can easily respond and upload their resume. Traditionally you would then read through countless resumés until you uncovered a group of potential candidates.

In order to save time, we install a hoop right at the very beginning of the hiring process that disqualifies applicants who cannot follow directions. In the body of the job description, we will give clear directions stating that in order to be considered for this job, you must submit your resumé at https://topclassinstallations.com/careers/. If you don't fill out the job application there, you will not be considered for this job.

I can't even begin to tell you how many people still submit resumes through the job board. Less than 1/3rd of the applicants follow the directions and fill out the application on our website. This proves to me that most people don't pay attention to the details and ultimately save my team time.

More precisely, when listing your services and offerings, be very clear on what it is that you do. If you look at the Top Class website, nowhere does it say, "We install car audio systems." It says, "We're on a mission to install GPS tracking and camera systems in 1 million commercial vehicles by 2025."

You need to be intentional in your marketing.

The reverse application of the 80/20 rule can also be applied to assess your existing employees. The way we do it here at Top Class Installations is we have a Google Sheet with our core values listed. If the employee possesses the core value at question, they score one point. We review each employee and ask, "Do they demonstrate this core value through their actions?" If they show this value at 50 percent or greater, they get a one. If they are less than 50 percent showing that value, they get a zero.

We use this spreadsheet to assess their core values once a quarter.

We have 13 values listed on the core values assessment spreadsheet that we use. Our seven core values are there, but we also have a couple of other values that didn't make the cut for our core values also included on that file.

Here's another great example of the 80/20 rule in reverse. Recently, an employee who's quarterly core values assessment dropped down to a score of 7 out of 13 has been the cause of most of the major bullshit that we've been dealing with at Top Class Installations. The data told me everything that I needed to know about this employee, and all I had to do was look at the score calculated by the quarterly core values assessment.

It's unfortunate, but now my business partner and I needed to make a tough decision. Is this employee further coachable? Or is he going to get cut from the team? And honestly, at this point in time, it's looking as if he's going to get cut from the team. We've already had a few discussions with this team member. It seemed that things were getting a little better, and ultimately, they have not. To drop from a 10 to a 7 is a really big deal for us. It's going to be a tough call, but you have to do what's right for your business and for yourself. Having to fire an employee is one of the downsides to owning and operating a business.

You have to have difficult conversations with people.

You can't let shit fester, because if you do, eventually you're going to get so pissed off that you're going to blow up. You're going to lose your mind, and you're going to become a complete animal. I mean, I know that's how it is for me, personally. As difficult as it may seem, you're better off being brutally honest with a person than not. Get it over with fast, and people will respect you for it.

Also, when you start looking at the lower 20 percent of these employees who are not aligning with your core values, it affects everything within your business. You also have to look at it and say, all right, how much is this actually costing me, keeping this ill-performing non-core-value-aligning employee on the team? Am I better off cutting this person quickly, now, and taking the hit? Meaning everyone's going to get a lot busier for the next couple of weeks until we find another hire. That's a major concern.

I look at hiring the same as a sales pipeline. You have to keep your pipeline filled with new hires and potential team members. So even if you're not ready to bring on board a new person, you have to have a couple of people lined up in that pipeline ready to go for you to pick from. Maybe it's someone who didn't make the cut three months ago when you were hiring. Call them back up. Shit, people change. They grow. Maybe their core values have changed. It's quite possible.

You should have your hiring pipeline filled at all times.

When you leave these non-core-value-aligning bad employees on your team, it costs you a shit-ton of money. I'll give you an example of how it negatively affects us here at Top Class Installations.

We're a service-based business, and we travel to the customer's location. Our technicians are mostly based in and around the five boroughs of New York City, Long Island, and New Jersey. If a Top Class technician performs a service at customer's job site or location and fucks something up or doesn't do the right job, we have to send another Top Class technician back onsite for free and fix it. I don't know about you, but I'm not in business to do work for free.

We typically cover a 150-mile radius from each technician's home base. That's pretty far. You have to figure that's at least a three-hour drive with no traffic. If you know New York at all, traffic is awful on most days, so it could be much longer than that. We recently sent two technicians up to Ravena, New York, which is just south of Albany. It's about a three-hour drive from most of our technicians, and they went up there to install a complex vehicle tracking and dash-camera system that was fully integrated. Meaning the tracking solution and the camera solution speak with each other and are able to be viewed on one screen, one software. The fleet managers of these vehicles can log into their fleet management software, see exactly where the vehicle is on a map, how fast it's going, determine if the vehicle is idling, track fuel consumption and much more. On top of that, they're able to click a button and watch the vehicle live as it's driving down the road. They can view the camera that's facing the driver and make sure the driver's not on his cell phone or is wearing his seat belt. Pretty cool technology.

This customer also requested a feature called Starter Kill. If you're familiar with car alarm systems, a starter kill prevents an unauthorized person from starting your vehicle even if they have the ignition key. Today's modern tracking devices are capable of triggering a starter kill. What I mean by that is the boss or fleet manager can go in from their computer or smartphone and click a checkbox and say, "enable starter kill." The next time that vehicle stops and shuts down if that checkbox is enabled, it activates an electromagnetic switch, called a relay, that we install in the vehicle. Even if the driver has the correct ignition key for the vehicle, once this relay is energized, you can't start the car.

We specifically sent these two technicians, who happen to be experienced, skilled Installers for Top Class. Both of them are really good, solid employees. But they each dropped the ball on resourcefulness, a Top Class core value. We sent these guys up there to perform these complex installs. They come back and tell us, "Hey; we can't install the starter kill relays because we're missing a cable." Okay. I have to take their word for it. I had done my research prior, and everything looked like it would have worked to me. But, again, I wasn't the one in the field. I wasn't the one touching and feeling the parts. Maybe I was wrong.

So, we ordered the additional cables; they come in, we send another technician from our team up there. Again, another three-hour drive to get to this customer's location. The technician leaves from Long Island early in the morning. Fuels up. He's got to go over two bridges and through multiple tolls to get to this location in upstate New York. Plus, all the drive time. Now we're not getting paid to go back onsite to do this work since we were already compensated for it and it should have been completed properly during the first visit.

Now the technician arrived on site for the second visit, looked over the parts and he says, "I can't believe it. These guys could have completed these installs." All of our technicians have a very specific cable, in their van stock, for another company we do work for. They could have pulled the van stock from that company, and the cable would have plugged right into this module. It would have given them the connection they needed to properly install the starter kill relays.

So instead my technicians completed these two installs for the customer, minus the starter kills. They said they couldn't do them because they didn't have the correct parts. Except, they did have the parts, they just weren't resourceful enough to look closely. They drove home. We ordered the suggested parts and rescheduled the customer for a second visit.

Our technicians could have completed the two starter kill installs had they looked a little bit deeper in their inventory. This lack of resourcefulness cost us hundreds of dollars in labor, travel, and parts. Worst of all, it unnecessarily inconvenienced the customer.

This is why it is so important to make sure your employees align with your company's core values.

Go to https://tomaskeenan.com/ and sign up for a free strategy session to kickstart your Core Value implementation.

Chapter 6: Vision, Mission, and Purpose

TOMAS KEENAN

◊◊◊

want to clarify what the difference between vision, mission, purpose, and core values are and how they all work together.

Your vision is comprised of three layers. The first layer is going to be your purpose, also known as your "why." The second layer is going to be your mission. And the third layer is going to be your core values. A Vision is necessary to have in place if you want to succeed in business. You can see an infographic that breaks down the different layers at my website, https://tomaskeenan.com/

Here is an exceptional example of a well-structured company vision by Keap.

Purpose:

We help small businesses succeed.

Core Values:

- We Own It: We are a culture of performance and accountability, and face challenges with grit and optimism to achieve our goals.
- We Learn Always: We have a forever-curious, learn-it-all mindset, and value learning over knowledge. We use data and experimentation to innovate and constantly improve.
- We Build Trust: We build trust through transparency and open authentic communication. We assume positive intent and are the first to extend trust.

- We Check Ego: We check our ego at the door. Humility and gratitude help us work collaboratively, serve others, and accomplish more.
- We Dream Big: We empower the entrepreneurial spirit by believing in people and championing their dreams.
- We Win Together: We are one team, unified in our Purpose and Mission. We all win when everyone does their part in service of the whole.

Mission:

Create and dominate the market of all in one sales and marketing software for small businesses with 100,000 customers worldwide.

As the business owner and CEO, one of your duties is to set the company vision and share it with the world. If you cannot clearly communicate and show people what your vision is, you're going to have a tough time succeeding. Picture your business as a ship in a giant ocean. If you have no vision, you're at the mercy of the sea. You will be aimlessly pushed and pulled in all directions by opportunities, life, finances, family, employees, ultimately lowering your chances of achieving your goals. By having a vision in place, you know the exact destination you must get to in order to achieve those goals. A vision allows you to enter the coordinates into your navigation and point your ship in the right direction.

One of the most difficult tasks we accomplished at Top Class Installations was to clearly define all three areas of our vision. We started with core values, then our purpose, and finally, our mission.

Your mission is simply what you do, who you do it for and by when.

Once we had the core values structured, it was pretty easy to get our mission outlined. Let me share with you our purpose and mission.

Top Class Installation's current mission:

"To install GPS tracking devices and cameras systems in one million commercial vehicles by 2025." As you can see, this does tell people exactly what we do, and it also has a goal built into it. So, the goal is one million vehicles by 2025. We've put an actual timeline on it. Now, since we have this date set on a calendar and know exactly what numbers are needed, this becomes a goal.

Top Class Installation's purpose:

"We bring efficiency to life."

When getting clear on your purpose, it's important to note that it's forever.

It needs to be able to outlive you and still be relevant 150 years from now. The Top Class purpose "We bring efficiency to life" is very fitting not only for what we believe in as a company but how we're forced to perform in order to stay profitable. In our line of work, we don't get to set the prices we charge since we're a subcontractor. Many times, we're bidding against another subcontractor firm for the work. We're told upfront if you want to work for us, this is what we're willing to pay you. Under these circumstances, the only way for us to be more profitable is to become more efficient. That's what fueled our desire to become more efficient in our early days, and now efficiency bleeds through everything we do because of the strong culture we have instilled throughout our organization.

Top Class Installation's seven core values:

Reliable:

We do what we said we'd do when we said we'd do it and the way we said we'd do it.

Quite simply if I tell you that I'm going to perform X, Y and Z action by X, Y and Z date you're goddamn right that I'm going to do it by the date that I said I was going to do it. If we book an appointment and I tell you that I'm going to have two technicians on site by tomorrow morning at 10:00 a.m. you better believe that I'm going to have two technicians on site by tomorrow morning at 10:00 a.m. If I tell you that I'm going to have a document emailed over to you within an hour you better expect that I'm going to have a document emailed over to you within an hour. If one of my employees tells me, "Tom, don't worry. I got this. I'll be on site tomorrow morning by 6:00 a.m.," that person better be on site by 6:00 a.m. tomorrow morning. If he's not, there's only a couple of valid excuses in the world of why he shouldn't be. But if you tell me you're going to do something you better do it. If I tell you that I'm going to do something you better believe that I'm going to do it. That is an unwavering core value. We're not leaning on this.

Coachable:

We check our egos at the door and are open-minded to possibility.

We've always found that if an installer comes into our organization, who has several years of existing experience, they are less likely to be coachable. Before we put core values in place, we hired solely based on skill. We would send a technician into the field after a brief phone interview to see if they possessed the skills needed to perform the work to our standards. Many of them were not willing to listen to our suggestions that would ultimately make them a more efficient and professional installer.

It's very important that each of our employees and my partner and myself are coachable. You just don't know it all. You never will. There's always somebody who's going to know more about it than you ever will. So, drop the curtain and just open your mind because there're people out there that are smarter, better, and faster at what you do no matter how good you are. You have to be willing to learn.

Resourceful:

We Google it first.

Our Field Technicians cover up to a 150-miles from their home on a daily basis. Sometimes we'll take a technician from Long Island and send them across the country for a two-week long project. That person has got to be resourceful. While on the road you don't have the luxury of a fully stocked installation facility.

You must have the ability to quickly overcome challenges without the help of others. You have to be able to pick up your phone and learn how to research things on your own. Don't bother me when you haven't even Googled the answer first. Don't bother me and ask me a question when you could've simply called one of the other technicians on the team.

I'm not saying my employees shouldn't ever call me when they have an issue, but they better have exhausted every effort before contacting me for assistance. If I'm answering the same question more than twice, I'm going to be pissed off.

Communication:

We practice open direct conversation.

If you have something to say, whether it's good or bad, just fucking say it already. I'm a big boy. I can handle it, and I expect the same from you.

As a business owner, it's important for you to not limit or hoard information from your team. You must have several channels of communication open at all times to effectively communicate not only with your team but also with those doing business and potentially doing business with you. Here are some of the tools we utilize to keep our communication flowing.

- Facebook Groups
- Slack
- Email
- VoIP Phone System
- Website
- Mobile forms app

- CRM
- Shared Google Sheets
- Loom
- Vimeo

Professional:

We look, act, and behave the part.

When you show up to a job site, and you're an installation technician for Top Class Installations, you better look professional. An acceptable outfit for my installation technicians: blue jeans, a Top Class t-shirt, a Top Class sweatshirt or jacket—all depending on the time of year and the weather. You have to be branded with your Top Class uniform. You must look and behave professionally at all times.

My office staff, for the most part, are all remotely based folks that are on the phone and shooting emails back and forth with our vendors and our customers on a daily basis. We must always look professional. We must always act professionally. This applies to the emails that we draft. Your grammar has to be appropriate. Your punctuation has to be correct. I can't stand when someone writes a text message, and they start giving you shortcode. Instead of typing the word you, Y-O-U, they type U. This is unprofessional. When people come into my organization, they better be professional. If you're not professional, and you don't match the core value, get the fuck out.

Caring:

We do the right thing.

As mentioned, several times already, my team is completely remote. We don't go into an office every day. My technicians are in the field. They're going to customer's locations. It could literally be three or four weeks in between times where I physically see a Top Class team member.

It's impossible to run a successful business standing over an employee's shoulder at all times; they must be a caring individual. You simply cannot be in two places at once. Whether I'm there looking over your shoulder or I'm in my office selling jobs, lining up work, marketing, networking, you have to be a caring individual. You have to do the right thing even when no one is looking.

When you're doing physical work on the vehicles, caring means your attention to detail. Make sure that your harnesses and your wiring are tight and flow nicely with the existing wiring put in place by the manufacturer. Make sure that you're working on that vehicle as if you owned it.

When you're speaking to a customer, treat them as if they're a loved one. You have to care for the customer, even if they're a pain in the ass sometimes. You've got to put that shit aside and remember, at the end of the day the customer is the one who is paying for your job, the tools that are in your hands, your automobile, your home, your food on the table, the clothing your kids are wearing. If you don't care, there is no room for you at Top Class.

Accountability:

We accept responsibility for our actions and the actions of our team members.

Let's face it; everyone makes mistakes. Your actions following your mistakes must be that of an accountable person. If a Top Class Installation Technician damages a customer's vehicle, they are expected to immediately notify the customer and our office. I don't want some lame ass excuse that later turns into more trouble or worse, cost more money to fix.

If one of our installation coordinators is entering customer information into our scheduling software improperly and a co-worker sees it, that co-worker is expected to speak up and help fix the issue before the problem escalates.

The reason that these seven core values work so well is that they apply not only to myself but to my business partner as well. It's a culmination of him, his personality, his beliefs, and me, my personality, and my beliefs, and what we stand for as individuals, and the togetherness of us in unity as co-owners of Top Class.

When Jimmy and I were hashing it out with our coach Dean, we argued from each of our points and perspectives of which are the values that we really stand up for, and what should transfer from our personal lives over to Top Class Installations? I don't believe that arguing is healthy overall, but it was a part of the process that we needed to go through to figure out who we are and what we stand for.

Whether you realize it or not when you have these successful and productive conversations with your partner in life, whether that's a spouse, significant other, a business partner, your core values are going to come to the surface

Jimmy and I wanted to put a core value in place around being on time. More specifically, always showing up on time to the job site.

Yes, we do agree with it, but at the core, we're not living it, although, I believe that you should never be late; you should always be on time. You should be 10 minutes early. If you're not 10 minutes early, you're late. But in all actuality, I don't live that; neither does he.

My business coach, Dean, called us out and said, "you guys can't put that in as a core value if you two aren't living it. It's like you're putting it on the wish list and you're just not doing it, so until you actually are living out that value you cannot consider it a core value."

As each session passed in Dean's office, we kept drilling down deeper and deeper and narrowing down the values that we believed in. At this point in time, I wouldn't even call them core values. I'll just call them values. After several weeks of going through this process of having these heated discussions that were necessary, we came down to approximately 13 values, and we put them on the whiteboard and asked, "Do you believe in this?" "Do you believe in this?" "Do you believe in this?" "Do you believe in this?"

We drew a basic matrix like an Excel spreadsheet on the whiteboard, and we laid out these 13 values on the top row. On the left-hand column, we laid out each employee's name, and then we went across, and we scored them. We asked,

"Does this tech have this value?" "Does this tech have this value, and this value, and this value?"

If the tech had that value, they got a one. If they didn't have that value, they got a zero. We did this for each employee on the team at the time. We then scored each technician on these values. This is something that we still do today. We've actually made it a little prettier. We've built a custom Google Sheet that we use to assess our employee's core values each quarter.

This was a very important exercise because it put actionable data in front of us. It allowed Jimmy and I to see where we currently were and where we needed to improve as a company. We immediately saw who on the team was not a right fit based on these values.

Within two weeks, we made personnel changes. It was a huge eye-opener, even though we weren't drilled down into our core values at that time; we were just at the value level. Taking this action was a huge deal for our organization because it gave us so much clarity and insight into who we are and where we could improve.

Chapter 7: Hire a Coach to Help You Get Clear

◊◊◊

I always knew there was more to business than what we were currently doing. Jimmy and I were just two technicians, literally in the field non-stop, working day and night. It's what we knew best, and it was comfortable. That's what we specialized in, and that's what we were so fucking good at. It was clearly working as we were making good money.

The problem was, as I started to realize since I was now expanding my family, I was never home.

All I could think was there had to be a better way to doing things.

So, I went on a journey to find a business coach. The first coach we hired wasn't anything fantastic, but I consider him the stepping stone that reignited my love of learning. He led me down the right path and forced me to read, which I needed in order to learn more about myself and business.

Our first coach suggested that we were at a point where we could use the structure of a CRM (customer relationship management) software system. He tasked me with finding the right solution that best fit our needs.

I spent over a month looking at hundreds of different CRM software before moving forward with Infusionsoft by Keap.

The whole reason I'm giving you this backstory of Keap here is they had, at the time, a network of local user groups that met up monthly. There was no added cost to participate in the monthly user group. I was all for it. I was and am all about making myself better. Besides, what did I have to lose?

I signed up for the group meetup, got in my car, and I headed over to this guy's office where the meeting was. I had no idea who these people were. I'd never met them. I had no idea what I was walking into. And sure as shit, I had trouble finding the location and showed up 35 minutes late. A wave of doubt and worry came into my head, and I tried talking myself out of knocking on the office door. "You're an idiot. You showed up late. Don't knock on their door. This is embarrassing." And just as I was walking up to the door, and I had psyched myself out of knocking on the door, this friendly looking guy comes over to the door and opens up and says, "Hey man, you here for the user group?" I felt like I was going to some 12-step program, almost ashamed. Like, "Yeah. That's me." And he says, "Alright, come on in."

When I walked into the office, I was blown away instantly. It was brightly lit, had clear branding, and company core values prominently displayed on the wall. Little did I know, this guy in his mid-30s, who answered the door, happened to not only be the co-host of the user group but also the business owner as well. I was like, *wow. This guy has his shit together*! I didn't realize at the time that all the office décor and branding was his way of infusing his company's culture throughout the facility. I was too naïve to realize that core values were part of his culture. To this day, I'm grateful for the warm welcome and how willing he was to help. I took an immense amount of information away from that interaction.

The following month, at the user group, I was introduced to Dean Mercado, the owner of Online Marketing Muscle. I eventually hired Dean to rebuild the Top Class website, and he also became my one-on-one business coach for over two years. I wanted to share with you the backstory of how life laid out these stepping stones for me. It's amazing how you start down a path, and somehow, the universe puts the right people at the right time into your life. Almost as if the universe is conspiring for you to win. These people had exactly what I was yearning for at the time. They had the knowledge, the wisdom, and the wherewithal to get me to where I needed to be as a business owner.

I couldn't get enough of the high-level information that was being shared, completely for free at these user groups. I would go and absorb as much knowledge as possible. If a group member mentioned a book to go read; I'd go read it. If a video was mentioned; I'd go online and watch it. If a group member showed us how to build a system or process within the business; I'd go back home, work until 3:00 a.m. and implement that system or process into my business immediately.

I met Dean at a local coffee shop to discuss working directly with him to help improve Top Class Installations. The first sentence he said to me was, "We're going to go see if we're a good fit for each other." I didn't realize it right there, but during his sales process, he was vetting me for my core values to see if I aligned with his. If my core values didn't align with his, he would've never offered his services to me as I wouldn't have been his ideal client.

I passed his tests. He said, "I'd love to work with you. There are a couple of things we need to do before we even begin."

Then he said, "If you want to work with me, your website sucks. You need a new one. It's going to cost you $6,000 minimum." I thought *I'm hiring this guy to be a consultant, a coach to me, and the first thing he tells me is you got to fork over $6,000 on top of whatever it is a month that I'm going to pay him for the one-on-one coaching.* That blew me away and scared me at the same time. Yet I knew it was the right move. We had a website at that point in time, but it was awful. After Dean explained everything in plain English to me, I understood that what he suggested made sense.

On Friday's I'd walk into Dean's office, go into the reception area, and he'd come out, and he'd say, "Hey, you want to go get a cup of coffee?" We'd go over to the kitchen area. He'd grab himself a cup of coffee. I'd grab a cup of coffee. And we would actually start our coaching session in there, usually with some small talk. "How're things going? How have you been? How's the family?" Just small talk while we made our coffee.

On this particular morning, Dean asked me, "How are you doing?" And I said to him, "Dean, mentally I'm completely fucked right now. We're super busy, and I have a lot of shit going on. I'm trying to get myself out of the field because I know I'm more valuable working on the business than working in the business. I'm having trouble finding somebody to go do the work at the same level and same ability that I can go and do the work." At this point in time, Dean had known me for quite some time and was always honest and upfront with me. And he said, "Hey man. I've been telling you for months that you need to implement core values within your business. Are you ready to listen to me?"

To elaborate a little bit more on this whole interaction with Dean that morning as we were getting coffee. When I told him that I was mentally fucked, super busy, and whatnot, my body demeanor said it all. I was drained, not standing tall, and had my shoulders slouched. Dean instantly read my body language and knew something was up. The real issue had been that we had three rotten hires that all happened back to back to back. That's when he came at me and said, "Tom, the reason why you're hiring the wrong employees is because you have no core values in place." That was when I fully realized what he had been telling me for months. I thought, *we really need to implement these core values into our business*.

As I went deeper into the rabbit hole, I didn't realize what the process would entail.

I figured, "Fuck. We'll just put core values in place and be done with it. Everything will be gravy." What I didn't realize was once the core values are established, you have to inject them into every fiber within your business. Your core values have to show up in your hiring process. *Like holy fuck, you need a hiring process? No one tells you that*. You think you can just look at a resume or application of the person interested in the job and, you say, "This one looks good. Let's call him in for an interview." Then you figure you'll sit down with him for five minutes, and say, "Come on in. You can start tomorrow." If you're doing that, stop. You're killing yourself. You have to put a hiring process in place. Core values and hiring all align. You have to hire the right way. Otherwise, you're costing yourself a shit-ton of money.

Once you start getting your core values narrowed down, you need to ask yourself two questions.

1. Do you really believe in the value?
2. Do you currently practice this value?

After several months, Jimmy and I narrowed our values down to 13 possibilities. It was still too many. We needed to get the number down below 7.

Having 10 or 12 core values becomes a lot to keep track of. If you can keep it between 4 to 7, that's probably ideal. Your employees are to memorize your company core values; if you have too many, this will be difficult.

Some of the issues that come from employees whose core values are misaligned from the company's are disruption: disruption to your production, disruption to your morals, disruption to your relationships. Disruption could be internal and external to the business meaning it could affect internal relationships between employees and management, and it could also affect your business externally — meaning customer-facing, client-facing, etc.

A bad hire is a tremendous financial burden to a business.

Go ahead and scare the hell out of yourself and Google how much a bad hire actually costs. You'll find spreadsheet templates that allow you to enter how much salary, ad spend dollars to advertising the job, training costs, uniform costs, and any other numbers that are relevant to the expense of onboarding and training a bad hire.

The numbers these templates spit out will absolutely floor you. You will realize: *that bad hire cost us $30,000 over the six months that we had him here*. I'd argue that guy probably cost you $100,000 and you just don't realize it yet. Figure out what a bad hire costs you, and if it hurts you as much as it hurt me, you're going to get clear on your core values quickly.

This will be obvious once you review the actual cost of a bad hire. The bad apples are just going to rise to the surface when you start going through these exercises and getting clear on your core values. You're going to be able to see with such clarity all the bullshit that you've been putting up with for so long that you didn't even realize it. Or maybe you are feeling the pain, but you are not willing to admit the truth until the facts are in front of your face?

I can't stress enough how important it is to fire quickly.

One of the ways we further filter applicants through our 7-Step hiring process is with an initial phone screening interview which asks specific situational questions. When answered, these allow us to see if the applicant's core values are aligned with ours. We'll weed out the bullshit based on their answers and intentionally force the applicant to jump through a couple of hoops. These typically are, filling out additional forms on our website, providing more detailed information about themselves, an optional 2nd phone interview, and time delay. Yep, we make them wait on purpose. We find that good hires are usually the ones who contact you asking about the application status. The next step is an in-person interview with 2-3 Top Class team members. We ask ourselves, "Could you imagine working closely with this person every day for the next 5 years?" If the answer is even slightly no from one team member, we cut them. If yes, we'll move forward with the hire.

If we feel that they are the right fit for our team, we'll offer them employment. They will be on probation for the first 90 days. What we found is usually around the two-month mark; sometimes sooner, people can't lie any longer. They can't put the fake face on anymore, and you begin to see their true colors.

The first time I met my in-laws, I was on my best behavior. Now, I can tell off-color jokes with my mother-in-law because we have that kind of relationship. Granted, we've known each other for a long time, but my point here is, in the beginning stages of a relationship, you tend to be on your best behavior.

I don't care how stringent and structured you are in your vetting process. They're going to show up dressed sharp; they're going to show up on time; they're going to show up with the car clean; they're going to show up with their tools organized.

Right around the two-month mark is when these people can no longer put their game faces on anymore. They can't hide behind the mask, and their true nature is exposed as they begin to get comfortable. At this point in time, it's our duty as employers to be aware of this transition. If you see that your new hire's core values aren't what you thought they were, you must cut ties quickly. The longer you wait, the harder it will be as you will constantly be second-guessing your decision. Indecision will cost you more money than the wrong decision made quickly.

Go to https://tomaskeenan.com/ and sign up for a free strategy session to kickstart your Core Value implementation!

Chapter 8: Roadmap to 1 Million

◊◊◊

I f you're a new business owner or you're just starting off in business, it's important that you stay hungry and most likely you are very hungry at this point in time. I'm not talking about food here. I'm talking about the fact that you're hungry to do any job. If something's thrown at you, you're going to gobble it up and just get it the fuck done.

I'm also a realist, and I understand that, especially in the beginning stages of a business, you need to do what you need to do to keep the doors open and the cash flowing.

At the same time, if I had known then what I now know about core values, my business would be in a completely different place than where it currently is now. I would be leaps and bounds ahead of where I currently am in business and in life.

Core values are necessary if you're going to succeed, last a long time, or if you want to build a legacy.

But business still has to operate. The business still has to make money. When you're first starting out and are the solopreneur, or you really don't have much help, set aside the time and hash out your core values. Make the time, take the hit today, so you don't have to take the repeated hits tomorrow and in the future.

You need to quickly understand as a business owner that you can't do it all yourself. You need to get help. That help can come in many different shapes and forms. You can hire; you can outsource. You can't look at outsourcing as an expense. I'm a trained car audio, car alarm, remote start installer. In short, I'm an electrician for automobiles by trade. I'm heavily trained, very skilled, and efficient at my trade. When I began marketing, sales, graphic design, accounting, and scheduling, I sucked at it. I was awful. I was not efficient. I had to learn quickly and repeatedly fail in order to get better. If I had figured out exactly how much I was worth per hour, it would have easily swayed my early decisions.

When you quickly add up that you're worth $250 an hour to your company, then you can assess, "If I build that marketing campaign, it's going to take me six hours. The end result is going to be okay. It might function, but it might not look the prettiest. It might not produce the best results." Then you can do quick math. 6 hours x $250 = $1,500. How much would it cost you to have that marketing campaign done by a professional? How much faster would it be completed? How much nicer would it look? How much better would it perform? More importantly, how much revenue could you have generated for your company if you focused only on tasks that you are heavily trained, very skilled, and efficient at?

It's important as a business owner and leader, to put KPI's (key performance indicators) in place. KPI's allow you to quickly monitor the health of your business. KPI's should be based on your goals. Your goals should align with your mission.

What's the overall mission of your business?

The mission of Top Class is to install 1 million tracking devices and Dash Cameras by 2025. *Okay. So, Tom, in plain English, what the fuck does that mean? Put a dollar sign on it for me. Tell me how much money that's going to turn into*?

We call this our Roadmap to 1 Million. Let me give you the numbers because they scare the living shit out of me. At the same point in time, I get super excited about them, and this is exactly how your mission should make you feel.

If we reach the summit of our Roadmap to 1 Million mission in the year 2025, that means in one year alone my team is going to install 356,000 tracking devices and dash cameras.

Money-wise, this will equate to an estimated $44 million dollars, and our team will have grown to 380 full-time employees.

Here's the Roadmap to 1 Million broken down into bite-sized chunks. Year one is a team of twelve. We installed 40,000 units that year. Our revenue was $1.4 million. Two years ahead, the revenue jumps to $3.3, employees to 28. The total units installed by the team is now 84,000.

That is a brief look at the Roadmap to 1 Million, and the numbers just continue to rise as the growth continues.

When you're setting your KPIs, break them down to yearly, quarterly, monthly, and weekly goals that need to align to your overall mission. As you monitor your KPI's, you can ask yourself: "Am I really where I need to be? Am I on track to hit my goal?"

A few years ago, I met a fellow business owner who happened to be a holistic doctor at a marketing conference in Phoenix, Arizona. We went out to dinner on the final night of the conference and had a great conversation about life, business, and family. It was a true conversation with someone that I quickly felt a connection with and admired.

We spoke about hiring people, how stressful it can be, and how it never seems to be the right time. He said, "Isn't it funny how every time you need to hire a person, there's seems to be no money. You say to yourself, how am I going to afford this? Yet you hire that person and almost magically the right shit falls into place. Suddenly you have more business that appears and helps pay this person's salary." I find that pretty wild and amazing.

Your business can't reach out further than what you personally can.

I'll give you an example here of exactly how this worked for Top Class Installations.

A few years back Top Class was comprised of 4 people; me, Jimmy, Juliana Chan, our Operations Manager, and Rob Felix, our Installation Manager. At the time, Juliana was coordinating and scheduling every installation for us. She was taking care of all the inbound leads via phone calls, emails, texts, and software portals provided to us by a few of our manufacturer partners. When a manufacturer partner would send over a job, Juliana would contact the customer and schedule the appointment with the end user. She would then assign and dispatch the work to the correct technician. We had a system. This system worked extremely well.

Opportunity arose as we landed a deal working with one of the world's largest GPS manufacturer partners. Obstacles surfaced quickly as this company didn't send us work via familiar methods. Instead of sending the work details and allowing us to schedule directly with the customer, they would call and say, "Can you get to ABC company tomorrow at 3:00 p.m.?" If you told them no, they would hang up and go find another installation company to perform the service at the requested time. Personally, I'm not a fan of this system, but it's what works for them. Therefore, if we wanted the business bad enough, we had to make it work for us.

Juliana had been telling Jimmy and me for several weeks that she was getting busier and busier with fielding calls from this large GPS manufacturer partner. To the point where this one company had inundated her with phone calls.

We decided, "All right, you know what? We need some help. We're going to hire another installation coordinator. That way Juliana won't be on the phone literally 10 to 12 hours a day. She can have some breathing room, and we can improve our efficiency." So, we hired another installation coordinator. Juliana developed the training process for the newly hired team member, onboarded her into the organization, trained her on our systems and processes, and magically, *we double our sales the next quarter with this large GPS manufacturer partner.*

I tell you the story because we were thinking small and in our own way. The lesson here is that you don't put the blinders on and say, *"only I can do it."* This is a trap, and I know it so well because I did it in my first business. I've done it my second business, and I still think to this day, part of me still wants to do it all.

As the industry expert who performs tasks so well and efficiently, it pains you to stop what you're doing to take five minutes and explain to someone, how to complete that task. In reality, they are going to mess things up a few times as they learn. As a perfectionist, this is hard. Especially when you're a business owner who knows exactly what you're doing and

---

In order to get out of or avoid the trap, you need to train people.

---

exactly what the outcomes should be. You're literally paying a person to fuck up when you hire them to take over a role or position within the business.

In order to train people efficiently, you need to develop systems and processes based on the role and daily tasks expected to be performed by the employee. You have to dedicate time in order to give people a clear understanding and expectation of what you want, and exactly what the end result will be.

At the same time, don't be a micromanager, instead, train yourself to tell them, "Here is the task. This is the end goal. This is where you start. Now, finish it." Let that person's inner genius come out. You cannot halt them. And, although you are the expert and you know exactly how to complete the task, you have to let somebody else own it.

When Jimmy and I first hired Juliana, we were scheduling, dispatching, updating, billing, and completing the installs. We were literally doing it all. Jimmy sat down with Juliana for a few days and slowly showed her our processes. He said, "all right, this is how you do this, and how you do this." Finally, one day she said, "Wait, this is asinine. You guys are doing things ass backward. Do you care if I do it this way?" That's how the Installation Coordinator roll was born.

At that point, we realized that Juliana had a solid head on her shoulders. She's an educated woman; she's smart; she communicates well with people. So, we told her, "If you've got a better way to do it, go ahead and do it. If it works well, update the processes. If it doesn't work well, fix it.

Has She fucked up? Sure. But who hasn't? That's part of life and business. People learn from their mistakes if you allow them to own the task at hand.

This is where systems and processes come into play and are so crucial.

I can't stress this enough, especially for these new guys starting out in business; whether you know it or not, you have a system. You know the steps in your head to get from point A to point B. If you're in sales, you know the sales process. You know what works and what doesn't work. If it's installation related, like my field, you know the steps required to properly install a tracking device in a vehicle.

The difficult and the time-consuming part is that you have to take a step back and document these systems and processes.

There's no excuse in today's day and age, not to create systems and processes. You can simply pull out the smartphone in your pocket and record a video. That's it. It doesn't have to be polished; it doesn't have to be perfect. Just record a video of you executing step A through step B. Then share it with people that come into your organization.

As you get more sophisticated, you can make checklists from the video. Then go back and watch the videos to realize *that step right there? Step three, it really isn't necessary. Why don't we eliminate that and streamline this process?*

If you document your systems and processes with video, you will be lightyears ahead of your competition.

Over this period, you're going to fine-tune the systems and processes that are your business. If you want tasks performed in a certain way, document them with video. Create a checklist and require them to be used. That's how you're going to show people exactly how you want things done while also holding them accountable.

You must leverage today's technology and capture your inner genius in order to show future hires how you perform tasks within the business. 99% of small business owners don't own businesses; they own jobs. They're unaware or unwilling to document in this manner and will stay small forever.

During our second year in business, we were awarded a 500-vehicle installation contract within the five boroughs of New York City.

At the time, it was me, Jimmy and occasionally one or two helpers. We accepted the project, and it took us almost three months to complete. Were we raking in cash? Absolutely. But we wound up neglecting our other customers as our bandwidth was maxed out. We could only do so much work in a given time frame. Our sales pipeline was full, but we were too focused on one customer to properly capitalize on additional opportunities surrounding us due to our first massive project. This is where systems and processes would have made all the difference. We could have easily bulked up the team and quickly trained new technicians.

Fast forward six years. I received a call from Jimmy, "Hey, we just hit a home run." A 6000-vehicle project that we quoted had just received a green light as was due to start in a few short weeks.

The daily installation quotas for this project were unbelievably high. In order to win the bid, we had to commit to completing 80 - 100 vehicles per day. We were given from June through August to complete the project.

What changed?

We were up to about 10 people in total on staff, maybe 11. But we knew we could handle it, because the systems and processes, had been built into the business by then.

We had found technology. We had implemented it in our business. We had put installation coordinators in place. We had people handling phone calls for us; we had people handling emails for us. We had people taking care of inventory. We had people prepping the units prior to going on site, so when the installation technicians showed up, they didn't have to prep the unit. All they had to do was install the unit into the vehicle and verify its operation.

We took the time and developed systems and processes for each of these steps.

Those systems and processes were the only reason the project was attainable and successful. Without those systems and processes, maybe we would have managed to pull the same numbers that we had done a couple of years ago, maybe we could have even hit a couple more as we became more efficient.

If you don't put the systems and processes in place, you're going to stay exactly where you are right now.

I do know this; there's no way we could've pulled off a job this size without our team, systems, and processes in place.

If you're happy with that, great. But I never settle; I'm never happy with what I have. I always want to make something better. Sometimes it's a fault of mine, but it's just the way I'm built.

In April 2014, the birth of my first daughter handed me the biggest dose of ass-kicking reality I had ever seen. My world and I instantly changed.

As a parent, you must be 100 times more responsible than you've ever been, at least if you want to be a good one.

At this point, my second business was a couple of years old. My first had failed. I knew how to work in a business; I knew how to be a good employee, but I didn't know how to efficiently run and grow a business. My daughter's arrival was the push I needed that forced me to learn more and become better at business.

I was working IN my business every day, but I had zero time set aside to work ON my business. Here are a couple of different examples of activities that describe working on your business versus activities that describe working in your business.

Sales is working IN your business. If you fulfill any sales role, that is work that you are doing IN your business, as an employee.

If you are driving to a customer's location to go check a vehicle, you're working IN your business.
If you are responding to emails from customers into the wee hours of the night, you're working IN your business.

If you're answering phone calls in the middle of dinner with your family, you're working IN your business.

Here's the difference.

If you are creating a marketing plan for the upcoming year, you are working ON your business.

If you are designing a checklist for your business, that's working ON your business.

If you're currently working with a business coach, you're working ON your business.

In your first couple of years, it will take some serious grit to get yourself out from behind the eight ball and let the world know who you are. While you will be doing a multitude of tasks, I merely want to let you know that there is a better way to run your business.

It all comes down to how willing you are to determine your core values, systems, processes, and training.

You know, it takes a shit ton of mindset preparation to be a successful entrepreneur and business owner. Most people think of a couple things up front when they say, "Oh, I'm going to go start a business. All right, I need a business plan. I need some capital, some money, and I need some ability to perform the actual work."

If you learn to leverage other people's time, you can be much more effective and efficient.

So, you might not have to be a total expert on whatever it is that you're getting involved in, but you have to know a little bit about it. And I'm here to tell you that there's so much more to it than that. If you want to have a successful business that's going to continue to grow and evolve, you must also grow and evolve with it. Your business is limited to the amount of personal development and the level of your existing mindset. So, if your mindset is stuck at level one, you can't expect your business to reach level 10. If you want your business to reach level 10, your mindset is going to have to hit level 10 before your business does.

Chapter 9: Mindset is Key

◊◊◊

Y ou have to work on your personal development and mindset for your business to grow. Without you getting better, your business will never grow; it will stay in the same place, and as Grant Cardone says, "If you're not growing, you're dying."

I have found reading to be a key component in shaping my mindset. It has caused me to continually push myself in order to obtain more success year over year. You need to constantly feed your mind with books. When I first started consuming books, it was difficult to read them due to the crazy hours I spent driving to customers locations and performing installs. To some, this would have been a deal breaker. Instead of making up some lame excuse, I turned to audiobooks and rapidly made my way through dozens of them.

There are so many self-help books available; just Google *Business Self Help Books*.

Not everyone is going to be right for you.

Sometimes the person reading the audiobook is monotone. You don't want to listen to them. You get bored, and you turn it the fuck off. That's fine. Move on. Get it out of your life and go consume something that you want to hear more. Go open a book that when you start reading it, you don't want to put it down.

But I do caution don't just be a consumer of the content. You have to step back, assess what you just learned, and then put it into action. I'm not saying to do every single thing that someone tells you to do in a book, but take a piece from this book, take a piece from that book, and once you've done that, once you've consumed all that content, you'll have ideas and you can then structure and reorganize the information to work best for you.

What got you where you are today, whether in life or business will not get you to where you want to go tomorrow. You're going to have to level up. You're going to have to readjust your trajectory; you're going to have to work on your mindset.

Everyone is different. You have to do what's right for YOU.

Here are a few more tips that will push you along in your personal and business development.

Write a list of the people currently in your life. Think about that person as an individual. Put people down like your mom, dad, brother, sister, crazy uncle, your neighbor next door, and best friend from high school. This is a list of the people who you spend the most time with. Whether you realize it or not, this list of people influences you and your decisions on a daily basis.

This has been said 1,000 times, 1,000 different ways and in 1,000 books. To succeed and grow, you have to surround yourself with better people and take the negativity out of your life. I am much more aware today where negativity stems from and of my surroundings.

You have to look at your friends and family closely.

You have to ask yourself, "Are these people positively or negatively impacting my life? Are these people negative? What content are they consuming? Are they constantly watching the negative news? Are they constantly complaining and talking about others? Do they blame others for their situations, or do they take responsibility for everything in their lives both good and bad?"

To reset your mindset and improve your chances of success, seek help from others who have already done what you're trying to do.

Once you have gone through the names on your list and have asked yourself these difficult questions, it will be clear to you who is negative and who is positive. The next step will be the hardest. You need to consciously limit your time with the negative people on your list.

There're several ways to do this.

Here is a list of activities that will supercharge your self-improvement:

- Read daily
- Practice gratitude
- Exercise daily
- Write down your wins daily, no matter how small or insignificant they may seem

- Hire a coach
- Listen to the Re-Wire podcast by Ryan Stewman

When it comes to hiring a coach, seek out someone who has already achieved the result that you want within your life and business. If the coach has not personally achieved the results you desire, move on.

You don't have to be the originator or inventor of an idea. If your coach has successfully accomplished the task at hand, simply copy what they did to become successful. And then, if need be, put your twist on it a little bit, but *somebody out there has done what you're looking to do already*. There's no reason to go reinvent the wheel. Study what that person has done. Follow that person on social media. Interact with that person. Hire that person as a coach or a mentor. *That right there is a short cut to success.*

Keep in mind you're still going to have to do the hard work. There's no way to avoid it but get clear now that you can get help from others. Don't be stubborn and say, "Oh, fuck this. I'll do it myself."

When you get help from the right coach, it will speed up your time to success.

Systemize and conquer

Jimmy and I went from doing everything, to slowly delegating tasks and jobs within the business to others. We began creating systems and processes to make it all possible.

There're a couple of steps here; I'll lay them out quickly and then we'll dive into them.

1. Take a personality assessment test.
2. Conduct a time study of your day to day activities.
3. Create a job ad and attract your first hire.
4. Implement a hiring funnel that automatically weeds out shitty applicants.
5. Extract your inner genius by recording videos.
6. Focus only on tasks you enjoy and are revenue generators.

I realized after several years that I'm not a doer. Don't take that the wrong way; I'm not a lazy person. I've done lots in my life; I have been very active. I've always been a hard worker. But what I've learned is I'm great at seeing possibilities and opportunities where others cannot. I'm a visionary. Once I have visualized a concept in my head, I can create it. Whether it's a marketing campaign or a custom interior panel for your '70 Chevelle. I'm great at kickstarting the initial project based on the vision, but when it comes to maintaining the project through completion and beyond, I fall short. To put it bluntly, my follow-through sucks, and my finishing skills are even worse. But I'm okay with that. I'm just being honest with the only person who really matters, and that's me.

Luckily, there are people on this planet who are excellent integrators. For you business owners and entrepreneurs, it's very important that you figure out if you are a visionary or an integrator. The difference is clearly defined and laid out well in a book called *Rocket Fuel*," by Gino Wickman and Mark C. Winters. If you want to really learn more about the differences, read that book.

The visionary is the one who comes up with a vision, who can put their head above the weeds and see out into the distance of what's going to happen in the future. The integrator is the one who takes the vision from the visionary and actually brings it to life.

Big difference.

So, I spent the first 15 years of my career as an integrator. I say this because I was a professional mobile electronics installer. I was integrating aftermarket electronics into existing electrical systems within automobiles. It began to cause major internal conflict as I learned more about myself and improved my mindset. I realized to move forward I needed to dissect my personality and figure out if the role of visionary or integrator suited me best.

Step 1: Personality Assessment

Take the free personality assessment test at https://www.tonyrobbins.com/disc/

The results are going to help you hire employees whose personalities work best with you based on your personality traits.

Your personality assessment will give you detailed information about who you are. Several key people within our company have done this, and it has made a difference in how we work as individuals and as a team. We started out as Job Owners, not Business Owners, and there's a big difference in those two positions. The personality test will help you transition from being a Job Owner to a Business Owner if you use the information the way it was intended.

When we hired our first coach, one of the things he had Jimmy and me do, was take a very in-depth personality assessment. It took about 20 minutes online, and within minutes, we had our results back. Which is pretty wild. I couldn't fathom how accurate it was going to be when I first took that test. It told me so much about myself, and so much about Jimmy. One of the reasons that Jimmy and I work so well together is that our personalities are complete polar opposites.

Where I'm strong, he's weak, and where I'm weak, he's strong. The assessment showed us the supporting data proving our suspicions.

Personality assessments are a great way to get to know ourselves and help deepen our understanding of others.

Here are 5 things you can expect to learn from a personality assessment:

1. Identify your strengths and weaknesses.
2. Identify your likes and dislikes.
3. How to best communicate with you.
4. What motivates you.
5. What situations allow you to perform at your peak levels.

After you take this personality assessment, take note of your strengths and weaknesses. When you bring on that first hire, look for someone who excels where you're weak. Finding employees who complement you and each other will help level out the personality differences across your organization and will allow you to scale faster.

Step 2: Time Study

Everybody is wasting time. There's a big difference between busyness versus business. I'm a failure in this aspect because I waste a lot of time with busyness. I know I do. If I could eliminate 10% of my busyness, and focus that on business, my revenue at the end of the year would be tremendously greater than what it currently is. What sets me apart is being self-aware of where my time is spent.

At the time of my first assessment, I was working more *in* the business than *on* the business. This wasn't clear to me until I completed the time study and saw the data with my own eyes.

I challenge you to complete the two-week time study outlined below. Once finished, you will have a deeper understanding of your self-worth. You'll become much more stringent on how you allow your time to be used. And, you'll have the content needed to create your first job description.

Start by breaking down your days into 15-minute intervals and documenting what you do during each interval. At the end of each week, separate the collected data into 1 of 4 buckets based upon how much revenue the task has or potentially will generate.

Bucket 1: $10 per hour tasks

- Data entry
- Answering emails
- Mowing the lawn
- Doing Dishes

- Cleaning your house
- Doing laundry
- Updating customers
- Confirming appointments
- Scheduling work
- Working as a technician within your business
- Driving to a customer's location
- Booking appointments
- Invoicing
- Collecting payments

Bucket 2: $100 per hour tasks

- Sales
- Marketing
- Managing employees
- Implementing new software into the business

Bucket 3: $1000 per hour tasks

- Any task that has you working *on* rather than *in* the business
- Designing Systems and Processes
- Recording Training Video's
- Working with a business coach
- Deciphering Core Values
- Attending seminars, conferences, and workshops
- Sharing your Vision

Bucket 4: $10,000 per hour tasks

Here is where you place tasks that bring value, but you can't put a price on.

- Spending time with your kids
- Date night with your significant other
- Exercising
- Public Speaking
- Going on adventures with friends and family

The overall goal here is twofold:

1. Determine where you're currently spending your time so you can begin delegating tasks that fall into the $10 and $100 per hour buckets. As a business owner, you want to get to a point where you're only working on tasks within the $1,000 or $10,000 per hour buckets.
2. Determine the roles and responsibilities of your first hire based upon tasks that fall into the $10 and $100 per hour buckets. These can also be tasks that you don't enjoy doing but are necessary in order to keep the business running.

What $1,000 per hour opportunities are you missing because you're too focused on $10 per hour tasks?

The time study's also going to be used to figure out what is going into the first hire's job description. Honestly, you should not be doing the tasks that you don't enjoy doing, and that you're not good at. Those should be the first ones that you get off your plate. Get somebody who's better than you, at completing those tasks, to do them.

Step 3: Job Description

Here is a sample of a well laid out and bulleted job description that is easy to read. This format has produced great results for us at Top Class.

Sample Job Description:

This position will be responsible for ensuring inventory accuracy for GPS and camera installation projects. The stock inventory manager will be working with logistics to coordinate receiving and picking up shipments following scheduling procedures and guidelines. The stock inventory manager will be responsible for ensuring the proper equipment and product are in working condition and hand-delivered to each respective location and/or installation technician.

RESPONSIBILITIES

- *Conduct routine inventory to maintain agreed upon levels of materials in stockroom*
- *Label incoming materials and complete documentation as required*
- *Use internal management system to ensure resources are available for upcoming projects, utilize Microsoft Excel and email*
- *Stock shelves and rotate stock with equipment that has been provided for installation projects*
- *Understand the overall supply chain processes and provide high level of customer service*
- *Deliver and pick up equipment/materials and submit orders for new product and supplies*

- *Complete selection and preparation of job-specific materials*
- *Work closely with team members and customers to determine appropriate stock levels*
- *Complete quality inspections on incoming materials*
- *Occasionally assist installation technicians on job sites for larger projects*

<u>REQUIREMENTS</u>

- *Applies acquired knowledge and skills to complete tasks*
- *Readily learns and applies new information and methods to work*
- *Communicates professionally with customers in person and via email*
- *Maintains a valid driver's license and reliable vehicle for transportation*
- *Works on routine assignments that require some problem solving*
- *Performs multiple tasks simultaneously, keeps accurate records, follows instructions, and complies with company policies*
- *Works under moderate supervision*
- *Communicates issues or problems to team members and supervisor*

Please email your résumé to abc123@companyname.com with the subject line "Stock Manager Job." If you fail to follow these directions, you will not be considered for the job.

Job Type: Full-time

Salary: $20.00 /hour

I recommend utilizing paid job boards.

You need to spend some money. The free shit doesn't work. Where you post the job depends on the role you're looking to hire. We've had better success hiring installation technicians from Craigslist and Facebook than from Indeed and Zip Recruiter. However, Indeed is our go-to resource for hiring office staff.

To save time and flush bad applicants up front, you need to create a hiring funnel. The sole purpose of the hiring funnel is to filter out the bullshit applicants. In my eye's, hiring is like marketing, except your applicants are your leads. Good marketing not only attracts the right people, but it also repels the bad ones.

If the applicant does not follow your strict criteria, they are eliminated instantly.

Here is an example of what we'd post to a job board:

Create and post the ad to the job board of your choice. If you've ever used any of these job boards, you know that the applicant can easily apply and attach a resume directly to the job posting. Don't use this feature.

Instead, list specific instructions in the body of the ad detailing how the applicant is to apply. For instance, we have an email address dedicated to new hires. That way, all new job applications come through to one specific email address.

Once you find an applicant who has followed your exact instructions, and who you think is going to be a good fit for your team and your culture, stalk them on social media. Look at them on Facebook, YouTube, LinkedIn, Twitter, Snapchat, wherever they are. What are they doing? Are they hanging out with losers? Are they clearly doing drugs, in the photographs that they're posting on social media? Are they posting dumb shit? If they are, that person's probably not the right fit for your business.

At this point, if you still feel the applicant might be a good candidate, schedule an interview. Get them on the phone to get a feel for their communication skills.

During the interview, you'll further assess the applicant's core values to see if they match up to yours. Ask situational questions that intentionally bring the applicants core values to the surface.

These situational questions are typically derived from situations you have experienced, or that occasionally happen during the course of business.

i.e.

- *You show up for your appointment, and nobody is there, what do you do?*

- *A customer is unhappy with your service and is asking to speak to your supervisor, what do you do?*

- *While servicing a vehicle, you find faulty wiring from another technician and an install that was done improperly, what do you do?*

You can see why you need to follow the steps I've laid out and get clear on your core values. Imagine how hard it would be to choose the right applicant without them?

The situational questions being asked during the interview will differ greatly depending on the role we're hiring for.

Now you should have a handful of candidates that have made it through the hiring funnel; you've narrowed it down, and you have to choose one candidate. Once you make that choice and hire the applicant, have them shadow you for a few days. Have the new hire write down the steps to each task that you complete throughout the day. After a few days, your new hire should have multiple checklist's ready for you to review.

Review the checklist and fill in any blanks or steps they might've missed.

Keep tweaking the checklist until you have a solid process for that task. What you're slowly doing here is leveraging someone else's time to document your inner genius. You're creating the systems and processes needed that will allow others to duplicate what you do and how you do it.

If you want to supercharge your documentation process, use screen recording software such as UseLoom.com. It's a free Google Chrome plug-in that captures audio and video from your computer screen. Simply record your actions while demonstrating the use of other software, writing emails, or social media posts.

Once you record your video, host it on YouTube or Vimeo as unlisted. This will keep it unsearchable and private unless you share the link with someone.

Once you begin to build your library, create a Word or Google Document that has a running list of all videos related to each role within your company. When you hire more employees, share the document with them. "These are the URLs for our training videos. Before you start your first day, you're expected to watch these videos. That way, you start your first day already knowing the lingo. You'll already know the processes and the procedures to do your job, without coming into work for your initial on the job training." This will shorten the required time needed to make this new hire a revenue-generating asset to your company.

Training videos are the modern-day operations manual for your business.

In today's day and age of technology, especially if you have a need for office staff, your employees can literally live anywhere in the world and still get their job done. We have one installation coordinator who splits her time between Florida and New York. I never know where she is. And honestly, it doesn't make a difference to me. As long as she has her computer, her phone, and an Internet connection, she can get her work done. Regardless of where she is in the country, her work is completed courtesy of technology...and courtesy of the training we've implemented. If I need to teach her something quickly, I record a video, send it to her, and instantly, she becomes a more valuable asset to the company.

This isn't 1985; you don't have to keep your documentation on paper.

Be proactive, start recording videos before you hire your first employee.

Then you'll have training information in place when that person comes in. Now, you don't have to spend three weeks recording all your day to day activities, because it's already done."

You can further systematize your processes and procedures if you have an assistant go through the videos and make checklists for you. If you follow the steps I've laid out, your business hiring process will have far less friction. Your business will grow at an exponential rate, and you're going to be able to do more than you ever thought possible.

Chapter 10: The Stepping Stones of Small Business Evolution

TOMAS KEENAN

◊◊◊

There're five stepping stones to scaling a business. They are:

Stone one: Open for Business.

Stone two: Staying Alive.

Stone three: Business as Usual.

Stone four: Get Ready for Takeoff.

Stone five: Exit or Expand.

Stepping Stone One: Open for Business

Your biggest hurdle is obscurity. Nobody knows who you are. You're new to the marketplace. Maybe, you have a small following of people, and maybe, you don't. You're wearing all the hats within the business.

You're responsible for marketing if you're doing any, at all, and most small businesses aren't. You're responsible for sales. You're responsible for fulfillment. You are the business.

The solopreneur, at this point, is either not fully committed, if this is their side hustle, or if they are fully committed, they're a one-man band. They're self-employed. Typically grossing between zero and $10,000 a month.

Stepping Stone Two: Staying Alive

Closing the sale is now your biggest hurdle. You might have an assistant or a handful of people working for you. Your revenue is between $100,000 and $300,000 annually. This is a critical stage.

Again, you're wearing a lot of hats at this stage. You're doing everything within your power to keep the business alive.

Stepping Stone Three: Business as Usual

This is typically where the operations, within the business steady out, and you begin to see traits in your data. If you're looking over your financials, you can say, "We're up' we're down." You'll have time and money to re-invest into the business, as well. Your gross annual revenue will be between $300,000 and $1,000,000.

Most companies, of this size, have been in business for a few years. You should be keeping accurate financials to tell how the business is performing. Employees range anywhere from 4 to 10, comprising one team.

The biggest hurdle while on stone three is the business tends to be perfecting their marketing and fine-tuning the actual services delivered to the customer (fulfillment).

Stepping Stone Four: Get Ready for Takeoff

Your business really starts to crank up. Employees range anywhere from 11 to 25. Sales are between $1M to $3M annually. The biggest hurdle you're currently facing now is hiring the right people and fine-tuning the systems and processes. Your team is ultra-critical to the overall success of your business.

Stepping Stone Five: Exit or Expand

This stage is the maturity stage of a business; you'll come to a crossroads and need to make a decision. Is this business going to grow? Is it still viable within the industry? Is it going to be profitable? Do we continue to innovate? Or do we, as the owners, sell off and get out?

At this point, the business is several years old. Sales range anywhere from $3M-$10M and up. You have a large team of people, anywhere from 25 - 100 employees broken into teams. You have multiple layers of management in place to run those teams. The biggest hurdle typically found in this stage is the continual infusion of vision from the leadership.

Keeping the culture strong and continually keeping the vision top of mind becomes increasingly difficult as your team grows. Now, if you're smart, when you're on stepping stone one, as a solopreneur you'll start working on the purpose, the core values, and the mission statement. If you do this right from the beginning, you'll be so far ahead of the game, that when it comes time to bring on people, that your business will expand and grow.

If you're struggling with implementing your core values in your business, Go to https://tomaskeenan.com/ and sign up for a free strategy session. Let's get you moving in the right direction.

Chapter 11: What No One Tells You About Business in the Beginning

TOMAS KEENAN

◊◊◊

W hat no one tells you about business when you're beginning, there's a lot of stuff out there that if you just jump into business right away, you're going to get smacked in the face really hard, and it's going to shock the shit out of you if you're not ready for it. I'm going to lay out some stuff here that you need to be aware of if you're going to jump in and go into business. Even if you have been in business for quite some time, you might not have experienced all of this. Here are a couple of things we're going to dive into. Alright?

There are incredible highs and lows when you are a business owner. You could be as high as a kite, literally, on whatever endorphins that are being released by your brain when you land a big sale; wrap up a large project, receive a recommendation, or someone praises you for what you've accomplished. It could be absolutely amazing, almost euphoric.

On the flip side, when finances are tough, when a customer puts you down, if a customer blasts you on social media—which eventually will happen—I don't care what business you're in, when your family is barking in your ear telling you this is a waste of time, when your significant other is pissed off because you don't have any money to bring in that week because you used what you made to cover payroll rather than your mortgage or put dinner on the table, those lows are real.

You must be aware that they're going to happen. They're going to come. They're going to get in your face, and they're not going to be easy to deal with. As your business grows, so do your problems.

Show me your network and I will tell you your net worth.

Your network is super critical. The people that you surround yourself with are going to determine what you begin to morph into. If you're hanging around a bunch of losers who aren't making any money that's pretty much what you're going to become. I had an uncle, and his famous statement to us as kids was, "If you hang out with horse thieves' people are going to think you're a horse thief." If you want to become a successful business owner or entrepreneur, make sure that you're hanging around successful people who have greater experience than you. The knowledge gained from these people will motivate, push, and propel you to get to where you want to go.

It's not easy to find someone willing to share secrets to their business success. If you want to expedite this process, be willing to spend money. Be willing to invest in yourself. Be willing to invest in the future of your business. Hire a coach. For more information, go to https://tomaskeenan.com/.

I believe that coaches are necessary. I went the first five years of my first business with no coach, and the first six years of my second business with no coaches. What we've been able to accomplish in the last four years of business, since investing with coaches, is unbelievable. Imagine if I had hired a coach in the early stages of my first business? That business might have survived. I might not even be talking to you about this right now. I might be on a different path in life.

Your coach doesn't have to be in the same industry as you. I'm a firm believer that business is business. No matter what you do, the same business principles still apply. If you're a roofing contractor and you meet someone who sells software, there's a lot of similarities to your business. You just don't know it. It's really helpful to have someone come in from outside of your industry put eyeballs on what you're doing, and then give you feedback. Because what works for them in one industry, even though nobody in your industry is doing it because no one's had that vision yet, might directly affect, impact, and work great within your industry.

Look to other industries and see what is working for them. If it's working there, chances are it will work for you, too. This is where you really need to set the vision. If you the vision is set, the path will create itself. In other words, you have to start with the end in mind. You have to be able to visualize the end of whatever it is you're setting out to do. Ask yourself, what is the end result that you want to achieve? Then work backward by reverse engineering the process.

Put in the work.

So-called experts are all over the internet, talking about taking a magic pill, and only working a couple of hours a week, to make millions. I've been in business long enough to know that when you sit back on your ass and do nothing, it might not affect you today, but it will affect you a couple of months from now. You have to put the work in. You have to focus. Don't go into business with the illusion that it will magically run itself and continue to produce high-level results.

If you want it to happen, you then need to build the correct team. You have to put the right people in place, and that takes time. You have to develop your hiring processes. If you're going to hire the correct people on your team, you need to identify and implement strict core values to filter people out who are not a fit. New hires need to align with the vision of the business. If they don't, find someone else.

Most people you come across are going to offer unsolicited advice.

Ideas without action aren't worth jack shit.

I'll give you a very quick story. I was at a customer's location a few years ago. He was a successful guy. We were talking about business when he said to me, "You know, it's amazing how everyone else loves to count your money for you."

That statement hit me like a ton of bricks because it was true.

Let's say your business grossed $1,000,000 last year. That does not mean that you profited $1,000,000 personally. By the time you pay taxes, employees, vendors, automobiles, fuel, supplies, and materials...hello? What's left? People see that you grossed a million bucks and they are like, *oh my god. This guy's a millionaire. He's rolling in the money.* Uh, no, I don't think so. That picture is laughable.

If you're a visionary like I am, you could literally have 100 new ideas in a single day. Most of those ideas are never going to come to fruition for a multitude of reasons. A) The idea sucks. You just won't admit it to yourself. B) You don't have the resources to get it done. C) Something else is going to pop up and be more important for you to do. D) You take no action and automatically fail. If you don't take action on the ideas that you come up with, they're never going to happen.

They're not going to magically appear.

As the visionary, you cannot let somebody else get in the way of your true vision.

If you know exactly what the end game is, and what that vision is, you cannot let somebody else's opinion or thoughts get in the way...especially when they don't have the clarity of the vision like you do.

Finally, family comes first. I've got three kids and a wife. Before my first daughter was born, I worked 20-hour days. I was constantly on the road and never home. It stressed my relationship with my wife, more than I know, but she did accept it at the time. She was also working full-time five days a week. We only saw each other on occasional nights and one day during the weekend. I had to do what was required to get my business off the ground.

What I didn't realize was that by focusing only on business, I was neglecting other equally important areas of my life, such as family and fitness.

Let's say, for instance, you start a restaurant. Let's just call that restaurant Glenn's Dinette. Okay? You're Glenn, and you own Glenn's Dinette. You start this restaurant, and you serve food. You cook, you serve the food, you clean the place, you order the supplies, you do the dishes, you do everything yourself. Over the course of the next 15-20 years, you hire a small staff to help you out, but nobody does things better than you. You have to be there every day, open and close; holidays, you're the only one who touches the register because you can't trust anybody. This right here is the perfect definition, in my eyes, of owning a job and not a business.

If you own a business, you should be able to step away from that business for a period of time, and that business should be able to operate without you, without your direct input. Don't take this the wrong way. This is so much easier said than done. This is the whole point of putting systems and processes in place and building these systems and processes so that your employees know exactly what to do when you're not around. Your core values tell your employees how to act based on the situation. There's a vast difference between owning a job and owning a business.

Set your vision and work toward it every day.

If you know that you want to own three restaurants, know what the end goal is before you begin. Do you want to sell them, or do you want them to run on their own after a couple of years? What do you need to do now to reach that end goal? What are you willing to sacrifice now in order to get there?

Yes, you might have to spend the first three years in the restaurant 20 hours a day, seven days a week, to get to your end goal. But you have to be willing to do that up front. Most people are not willing to do what's required. Get clear on your vision. Think it through because it's going to affect all areas of your life.

Take some time to reflect and see if your current actions, or inactions, align with your core values. *Is the decision that I made to start this business in alignment with my core values? Is this decision to leave my job in alignment with my core values? Is this decision to take on this new customer in alignment with my core values?* These are the kind of questions you need to continually ask yourself as time goes on. Never stray away from these questions because your core values are your guiding light. They're going to be the answer to all of your deepest, darkest questions, to all the shit that's been bothering you forever.

Keep asking yourself these questions, and eventually, whether consciously or subconsciously, you'll come around and give yourself the right answer.

TOMAS KEENAN

Chapter 12: Goal Setting

◊◊◊

Goal setting is a topic that's had a ton of coverage by many people before me. I want to give an overview of what you should be doing in order to properly set a goal.

The first thing you need to do when setting goals is to make sure they're SMART.

- **S**pecific
- **M**easurable
- **A**ttainable
- **R**elevant
- **T**ime-bound

How to write SMART Goals

1. Specific

All goals should be clear and specific. A stranger should be able to know your exact intentions by reading them.

Ask yourself these questions:

- **What** exactly do I want to accomplish?
- **Where** is it located?
- **Why** is it important?
- **Who** is involved?

2. Measurable

"What gets measured gets improved." Peter Drucker

Measurable goals allow you to track your progress.
Ask yourself these questions to ensure your goals are measurable:

- How much?
- How many?
- How do you know when you've accomplished the goal?

3. Attainable

In order for Goals to be successful, they must be attainable. Be realistic with your goal setting but make sure you stretch your comfort zone. You don't want goals too easy to achieve. Make your goals big enough outpace your competition even if you fall short of attaining your them.

An achievable goal will usually answer questions such as:

- By what means can I accomplish this goal?
- How realistic is the goal, based on outside restrictions?

4. Relevant

Your goals need to align with your core values and overall mission. The real power comes when you have goals that overlap. For example: Goal A can only be achieved by completing Goal B.

Ask yourself these questions to ensure your goals are relevant:

- Does this goal align with our purpose?
- Does this goal align with our mission?
- Does this goal align with our core values?

5. Time-bound

If your goal doesn't have a target date set, it's not a goal, it's a dream. Every goal needs a date marked on the calendar. Once a date is set on the calendar, it becomes real.

Questions to ask:

- When?
- What do I have to do monthly to complete this goal on time?
- What do I have to do weekly to complete this goal on time?
- What do I have to do daily to complete this goal on time?

If your goals are not in alignment with your core values, you're going in the wrong direction, away from your own deep sense of purpose and passion.

When your goals are aligned with your core values, you're going to feel more energized and engaged, and you also have increased confidence knowing that you're moving in the correct direction of your true authentic self.

Now, a word of caution: Just because you align your goals with your core values doesn't mean that you're going to eliminate inevitable challenges or bumpy roads in life. Let's just get real. No matter how amazing somebody looks on the outside, nobody gets a free ride.

But bumpy roads are more manageable when you're going in the right direction. The bumps are a part of your process, and they need to be expected.

You're going to encounter them regardless of if you have clearly defined core values in place or not. But if you have the core values and the goals tied to the same mission, you'll manage those bumps in the road with ease.

Nobody gets a perfectly smooth road to go down.

Tony Robbins said it best: "If you talk about it, it's a dream. If you envision it, it's possible. But if you schedule it, it's real."

I suggest you read an awesome book called "Essentialism," written by Greg McKeown. This book is about getting more done with less because we're focused on the right goals.

Focus on one or two goals and watch yourself gain incredible traction and go the distance on those goals rather than go a smaller distance on 10 to 20 goals.

That makes a lot more sense, doesn't it?

Chapter 13: Feedback vs. Chatter

◊◊◊

Seek guidance and feedback from those who you look up to, those who have accomplished what you're striving to accomplish in your life now.

What you are hoping to do is demystify your own perception. To do so, you must be willing and open to receiving feedback from others. Thicken up your skin because some of the information that will come back to you, you're not going to like. You might hear something negative about yourself, about your personality, about your mannerisms. It might dig up old shit that you've been through with somebody in particular or a group of people; you might have to face history that you're not so proud of.

Face it now. Get that crap out of your life.
Crush it. Move on.

You're most likely holding on to limiting beliefs deep within your subconscious. You need to talk about and clear them out. You need to extrapolate these limiting beliefs from your brain, and your subconscious so you can move on and become the person you are destined to be.

Understand there's a difference between valuable feedback and chatter. This is why you need to identify and only target the correct people who are going to give you valuable feedback. This is why your network is so important. I'm not saying target people who are going to give you the feedback that you want to hear. I mean, find people within your life who are brutally honest, upfront and to the point. Open yourself up and become receptive to constructive criticism. This is not a blow to your ego. This is the kind of information you need coming back at you, to help determine where you are, and if you need to make a change.

The beauty of defining your core values now is that over time, you will grow as a person, and as your business grows, your core values most likely will change. Mine have. In fact, since the first time I did the exercise until recently, they were very similar, but some evolved.

Change in life and in your core values is okay because you're going to evolve as a human.

You're always going to be learning. Every day, you will absorb information and stimulate growth. Your thoughts will change. The way you look at the world will change.

As you level up, and you surround yourself with winners, you're going to look out into the world through a clearer set of lenses. When you do, you're going to see problems resurface as opportunities.

Chapter 14: The Fear of Letting Go

◊◊◊

'm going to talk about the fear of letting go. Letting go is one of the hardest things to do. As an entrepreneur, as a small business owner, it is an incredible challenge because you, the technician, know and understand exactly what to do within your business. You know all the answers because you are the only one. If you don't know the answers, you know how to get them because you're resourceful.

When begin to hire employees, a major problem is going to come to the surface, it's going to bubble up, and you need to cope with it. If you plan on being a one-man show, a solopreneur, for the rest of your career, then this need not apply to you. But for those of you who are looking to build a business, build an organization, leave a legacy, you're going to need to get very comfortable and used to allowing others into your organization, to start taking over the tasks that you are doing on a daily basis.

Again, this all goes back to your time study, and $10 an hour tasks versus $100 an hour tasks versus $1000 an hour tasks. I don't think it's wise for you, the business owner, to stay focused on $10 and $100 an hour tasks. At some point in time, if you want to get bigger, better, you want more materialistic things, you want a better business, you want more time with your family, then you're going to have to learn to get comfortable with delegating, and let others take over menial tasks for you.

In all honesty, if you're having trouble letting go, you're just adding friction to the growth process. You are literally standing in your own way. Here are a few different scenarios so that you can better relate. As experts within our business, we all have a tendency to micromanage.

What you have to do is, and this is really tough, and I'm just telling you from firsthand experience, you can't delegate work and ask 600 times once you've delegated the work, "Where are we on this? How are you doing? Anything I can help you with?" You have to put trust in the person that you handed that work off to.

When you micromanage your business, and those who work in your business, you become the bottleneck.

You can't make the processes within your business completely dependent upon one single person's answer because if you do, you're going to have to jump into every single project there is within your business, and your time is more valuable than that of your employees. When you do this, you will lose your time, and time equals money. Your time is better spent looking ahead and working on big-picture items such as your purpose, your mission, and focusing on core values. If you focus your efforts on your vision rather than the minutia within the business, not only will you go further, you will go further faster.

One of the main struggles we had at Top Class when we were first getting started was letting go and delegating. Our first hire was an installation technician. Since our business requires an installation technician to travel to the customer's location, this becomes a challenge because it gets to a point in time when you can't physically be there with the installation technician and look over their shoulder and ensure that they are doing the right job every time.

You can't be in two places at once, but if you're ever going to scale, you have to develop systems and processes to hold your people accountable.

Micromanagement kills productivity, morale, and the potential of your employees.

Being a small business owner or an entrepreneur is like living on the world's biggest rollercoaster. At one minute, you're at the very top; it's amazing, you've never felt better; you just sold a big deal; you just finished a big project; you just landed a magazine article; you just were interviewed on a podcast; you just met somebody famous and signed them. But literally within a flip of a switch, you could be at the absolute bottom. You could be depressed and down on yourself. Being an entrepreneur, a leader, a business owner, can be a very, very lonely place.

You can't bottle up all of these emotions within you without some form of an outlet. I know a lot of entrepreneurs probably get into some outlets that aren't the best for them, maybe drugs, or alcohol, but there's got to be a way for you to get these emotions out of you in a positive manner.

Here are a few that have worked for me:

- Exercise.
- Schedule time to be away from the business and just think.
- Disconnect from technology.
- Find a hobby and put it on your schedule.
- Get your spouse involved in your learning. Take them to conferences with you. As you grow, they grow. This will keep you closer and relatable as the years pass.

Getting through the lows ties back to having a solid morning routine. You have to stick to it. Over the past 10 years, we've had our ups and downs and still do. Every day a random fire pops up. But you have to find ways to cope with it that are not going to be detrimental to yourself, your health, your family, or your partnership. For me, what's been super helpful is getting up early daily, and following a strict morning routine.

Your morning routine sets the tone for your day. You win or lose in the first 30 minutes after you open your eyes.

I get up at 5:30 a.m. It might sound early to some of you; it's super early to me because I'm naturally a night owl, always up to 1:00, 2:00, 3:00 in the morning, whether it was working or partying. When I did that getting up at 9:00 or so wasn't such a big deal.

Immediately upon getting up, I put my AirPods in my ears and listen to a positive podcast, or YouTube video. I have a list of people that I follow and listen to, pretty much daily, I devour their content and what they put out to the world.

Then, I drink a big glass of water, wash my face, brush my teeth, and now, I'm awake. The next stop is the gym. I can't stress enough how important it is to get your body moving early in the morning. Go for a run or a walk; ride a stationary bike. You have to push your body and make yourself sweat a little bit in the morning.

From there, I head home, take a shower, spend time with my kids and then I head into my office and I do a couple of things. I write every day, for instance. You don't need to write as though you're writing a book, although you could incorporate that if you want to. Write down your thoughts, where you are, your goals. Record where you are with your goals. Write down 5 things you are grateful for.

If you guys follow me on social media, I post positive content almost every single morning. That's me putting out my positive vibes and messages to the world.

Next, meditate. I use the app Headspace, just plug in, and try to get 10 minutes or so in a day on Headspace. Quiet your mind. Go over your core values. Look at them. Read them out loud. Look at your goals, again; read them out loud.

At the end of the day, I look at my goals, read them out loud, look at my core values, read them out loud. Then as I lie down in bed, I put my head on the pillow, close my eyes, and I focus on visualizing the future. I visualize not the next day, not what's going to happen at work in a few short hours; instead I focus further into the future.

Visualization is so important. Where are you? What's the weather like? Who's in the room? What colors are the walls? What color is the carpet? What pattern is the carpet? What are you doing there? Who are you with? What do you smell? Let go, relax, and let your mind wander. Those visions will become a reality if you focus on them enough.

The reason you need to structure a morning routine is to get the hardest and most important work done first.

That way, there are no excuses for you to not get them done later when you're exhausted from the day's activities and challenges. You need to work on building faith within yourself.

I'm actually in better shape now at 40 years old than I was at 25, but if you neglect things, they will come and bite you.

Go to https://tomaskeenan.com/ and sign up for a free strategy session to kickstart your Core Value implementation!

Chapter 15: All Business Struggle at Some Point

◊◊◊

A couple of months back, we were tight on cash at Top Class Installations. When the finances get tight, and you have responsibilities such as payroll for multiple team members and those team members rely on you to pay them on time—and if you don't pay that person, you're going to fuck them, and you're going to possibly fuck up their marriage, their family, their children, them putting food on the table, them covering their personal bills. It's an enormous responsibility to employ people, and it's one that I do not take

---

All businesses struggle at different points in time.

---

lightly at all.

In my case, we had just come off a killer year, and great projects where cash flow was very good, then we got involved in a shitty project that didn't work out for a multitude of reasons. One thing led to another, and we weren't as busy as we should have been.

When these situations arise, we tend to be a little bit more lenient in what we're willing to accept, and this is the problem. This is where the shitty situations develop, and if you're not careful, they grow worse. That's exactly what happened. My partner and I were, scrounging, doing whatever we could to do to go out and sell jobs and get that money in. I had recently started a private Facebook group for the GPS tracking installation industry. If you want to go check it out, just search "GPS Tracking Installers[4]" on Facebook, and if you're in the industry, apply, and maybe I'll let you in. I connected with a person in that group who was in need of help and looking to hire another installation company. This person also owned an installation company and had a large project in our area and asked us to assist.

The first couple of words of the conversation were, "I need this done extremely cheap." When you're in a situation where your finances are tight, and you need to make payroll, you tend to accept things that you normally wouldn't accept. You tend to be more lenient. We accepted an installation price that was literally a third of what it should have been. The good part about it was that it was a bulk job, meaning it had a lot of volume behind it, but the overall pay was just not where it needed to be. We accepted it because it was guaranteed work for a couple of weeks, and it would have been enough work for multiple technicians.

It would have covered payroll for four technicians for six weeks. As we worked on it, several problems arose. The end user was not providing the daily number of vehicles as promised. The end user was not putting all of the vehicles into one centralized location; my installation crew was walking miles per day in big lots looking for vehicles, sorting through keys, and then driving to multiple job sites to get the work done, which decreased efficiency further.

We thought we were making $40 on that particular install per vehicle but then had to calculate all of the time wasted traveling to and from locations looking for vehicles and it

---

[4] https://www.facebook.com/groups/gpsti

turned out we were making $34 a vehicle. That makes a big difference over a large deployment of multiple vehicles. When you have a job for 1500 vehicles and your losing $6 a pop, that number adds up pretty quick. These were the problems that started off the first week.

We had set a net-30 payment term with the other installation company who had hired us. Which meant they were going to pay us within 30 days of completing the work which is pretty standard within our industry. We are relying heavily on this money at this point in time, and 30 days comes and goes, 40 days comes and goes, 50, and 60 days comes and goes.

Now, this whole time, Jimmy and I are trying to collect this money as if our business depended on it, and it did. Our business was not doing well financially. We didn't have enough work coming in to pay our team.

We had to leverage a line of credit to cover our expenses and payroll for the next couple of months. On this one project we let our guard down; we didn't put this person and their company up against our core values and assess if they would have been a good partner from the get-go; we let this person into our inner circle, and they damaged our company for several months.

You have to step back sometimes especially in stressful situations.

Bad financial situations tend to be the most stressful situations you encounter. When you're in those situations, you need to step back and think before you act.

Think before you commit.

We would have been better off denying the job this person had offered us.

Not all business is good business. Hopefully, when you implement core values into your business, you're going to use them on a daily basis, and you'll be able to determine quickly if the business "opportunity" is a good fit based off your core values. Remember, not every opportunity that is offered to you is a good opportunity.

Here is a great opportunity to better your business

Go to https://tomaskeenan.com/ and sign up for a free strategy session to kickstart your Core Value implementation!

Afterword

One of my biggest fears with this book is that you will not take action on what was outlined in this book. If you take no action, you get no results. I've been to several business conferences and masterminds during my career. I don't want you to read this and do nothing because I equate that to being a conference junkie. That's the person who goes to 7, 8, 9, or 10 conferences a year and does absolutely nothing with the information that was presented to them.

I see people that pay good money to attend these high-level conferences and don't implement anything that they learned while there. The first thought that goes through my head is, *why the fuck did you go to this conference if you're going to go home and not do the work? Did you just go to spend the money and write it off as a vacation?*

I value my time way too much. That goes along with the values we put into place. That goes along with the purpose of Top Class Installations—bringing efficiency to life. Don't think: *hopefully, by osmosis, I'll just get this information and magically my life's going to get fucking better.* No, you have to do the damn work.

Core values won't magically enter your life and make you a better person. You're going to have to actually take some time; you're going to have to physically put pen to paper and write down your intentions to get clarity on yourself and business.

Without action, you're just the asshole who went to the conference and didn't even take notes while you were there.

Acknowledgments

I want to mention by name a few people that have made a significant impact on my life, and I am forever grateful for them.

I can't wait to see what the next chapter brings for all of you.

Ryan Stewman

If I hadn't taken the risk and invested in your coaching programs, I would have never been introduced to the people in your network. In this vast network of amazing people, I was quickly introduced to Hilary Jastram. Due to the support of the APEX family, it was easy to determine that not only did I want to write a book, but it was possible.

When you surround yourself with experts and winners, doing what you once thought was impossible becomes quite easy, if you're willing to put in the work.

You have taught me to focus on the supporters and not the reporters.

For you, I am forever grateful.

Hilary Jastram

You are one of the kindest, most uplifting and positive people that I have ever had the pleasure of surrounding myself with. Your innate coaching abilities, patience, and belief in me from day one was nothing short of amazing.

Because of you and your kickass team, I will proudly tell the world that I'm an Author.

We're not done yet...

Kathryn DeHoyos

We connected through Hilary but quickly bonded on another level since we're both parents of twins. The years of experience, knowledge, and passion you have for writing cannot be denied.

The long hours you put in daily, not only on the home front but in your professional as well life tell me all I need to know about you.

About the Author

Tomas Keenan is best known for his humble beginnings and lengthy career as a custom car audio installer. He is the epitome of a technician turned CEO. Tomas is the co-founder of Top Class Installations, an industry-leading GPS Tracking, and Dash Camera installation provider. He and his team are on a mission to complete 1 Million installs by 2025.

After gaining massive success in running and operating his mobile installation company, Tomas decided to teach people from other industries how to create their own success by building their own service-based GPS installation businesses. Tomas' transparent communication style has helped over 500 telematics industry colleagues succeed in business.

His expertise and vast experience have put him on the pages of the top industry magazines time and time again. He has been featured in Mobile Electronics Magazine, CE Outlook, CEO Blog Nation, Fit Small Business, The Startup Growth, and several Blogs in addition to countless podcasts.

He states, "The key to his success is making progress every day regardless of how small it may be."

Tomas was born and raised in New York. He's a devoted husband and proud father of three amazing kids, including a pair of twins. Outside the office, Tomas enjoys bow hunting, playing with technology, sharing new experiences with his children, and stretching his comfort zone. He and his family live on Long Island.

Subscribe to his blog at https://tomaskeenan.com/

Made in the USA
Middletown, DE
17 April 2021